The Life of a 1970s Teenager

The Life of a 1970s Teenager

Todd Bueler

TAB Books Toronto

Copyright © Todd Bueler 2025

All rights reserved under International and Pan-American Copyright Conventions. No part of this book may be reproduced in any form without permission in writing from the publisher, except by a reviewer, who may quote brief passages in a review.

Published by TAB Books – Toronto

This is a work of creative nonfiction. The events are portrayed to the best of the author's memory. While all the stories in this book are true, some names have been changed to protect the privacy of the people involved.

Editors:
Nancy Bueler
Beth Rodgers
Marcia Drummond

Cover Art: Jake Bueler
Author and Rear Cover Photos: Nancy Bueler

Main Map Illustration: Cameron Ojeda
Other Map Work: Todd Bueler

Set in Georgia 10pt typeface – Matthew Carter, designer

Library and Archives Canada Publication Data

Bueler, Todd A., 1962–
The Life of a 1970s Teenager

ISBN 978-1-0691536-0-9 (Paperback)
ISBN 978-1-0691536-1-6 (eBook)

First Edition – February 2025
10 9 8 7 6 5 4 3 2 1

Dedication

For my children, Grace and Jake. I never knew anything about my parents' youth or their teenage years, so here is mine. Here are all my loves, losses, triumphs, sacrifices, and struggles, as I navigated the 1970s as a teenager and beyond.

Contents

Foreword	v
Author Preface	viii
Maps	
Swansea - Main Map	xii-xiii
Riverside Drive	21
Run From Cops	192
Swansea - Micro Neighbourhoods	240-241
Introduction	1
Earliest Memories and Moving to Swansea	1
First Memories of Swansea	6
Ya Little Puke	8
The Neptune Factor	10
I'm Down Here!	11
I Warned You!	14
House Party on Lavinia	16
The Poke Check Kid	18
Riverside Drive and the Big Rec Room	20
The Tom Trilogy	26
A Game of Muckers	26
This One's Hot	28
Championship Ping Pong	30

Swansea School Funnies - Grade 6	**32**
Part I	32
Part II	33
Waking Up! Detention Time	**35**
Writing Lines	36
Gym Class	37
Awake	38
Contentment	39
Walk Out on Your Hands	**40**
A Little Quick Money	**42**
The Greatest Gig	**44**
A Weekend at the Swansea Rec Centre	**48**
Moonshine, Vodka, the Cops, and the Dance	49
My Mom's Car, More Cops, and a Narc	53
A Morning Punch and an Afternoon Slap	59
Summertime Hijinks	**64**
I'm Not Getting in That Trunk	66
Mooning the Humber Theatre Crowd	68
They Took Our Clothes!	69
True or False - Part I	**72**
41091	**74**
Vic Edwards and his Mom's '59 Vette	**76**

Booted Out of School for Good at 15	**78**
Why?	79
Clean out Your Locker	80
Walking in the Rain and Animals	83
The Working Life of a 70s Teenager	**87**
Then Along Came Sophie...	92
Nancy	96
Pool, Billiards, 8 Ball, 9 Ball and a Hundred Bucks	**109**
Playing Pool at the Swansea Rec Centre	110
The First Hustle	111
The Protocol	121
Protocol Points	124
The Pool Hall Hustle	126
The Chase	133
That Creepy Old T-Bird	**145**
Creepy Old T-Bird Explanation	147
The World of a 70s Teenager	**148**
I Don't Believe You	**154**
Mercury Blues	**158**
A Window with a View	**161**
That Night I had a Dream	163
My '78 Gibson Les Paul	**165**
Tell Me Why I Shouldn't Take Your Licence	**168**
True or False - Part II	**171**
High Roller Baby	**172**

The Vodka and Oranges Urban Myth	**180**
Holy Shit. It's the Cops! Run!	**185**
Dreaming Again	197
The Rolling Stones	**200**
The Postman Gets Knocked Down Twice	**202**
Return to School	**207**
College, a New Baby, and Poverty	**213**
Never Judge a Book by Its Cover I	**220**
The Joys of Having Children	**222**
Never Judge a Book by Its Cover II	**223**
My Dad	**225**
Pong	225
One Froggy Evening	226
Other Writings	**227**
Leaving School at 15	227
High Strangeness in Swansea	228
The Brain Tumour Incident	230
The Postman Gets Knocked Down - Why Write It?	233
Appendix A - The Coochie Dome	**236**
Appendix B - True or False Answers Part I	**238**
Appendix C - True or False Answers Part II	**239**
Appendix D - Micro Neighbourhoods	**242**
Appendix E - Swansea School Report Cards	**244**
Acknowledgments	**248**

Foreword

I was a school teacher for almost 30 years, with 17 of those being at the public school in Swansea, Toronto, where this book is set. I taught both Todd Bueler's children while at Swansea Public School, and met him on a personal level after I retired from teaching and became a writer. I had just published a book on the history of Swansea School when Todd was beginning to write his book, and we would meet on occasion in the neighbourhood for coffee and to talk about writing. During one of our meetings, Todd went into some details of his book, saying how he had lived in Swansea his whole life, a rare thing these days. I mentioned that I felt that would give credibility to his writing. After reading the finished manuscript, I found I was correct.

Last summer, I was out driving with my son. When we came to a certain bend in the road, I told him how the highway we were driving on used to be a farmer's field. He pretended to be interested for a second or two, and then looked down and checked his phone. Okay, he's not that interested in my old stories. Am I just not telling them right? Are they too blandly nostalgic? To be fair, I guess it did make me sound like an old guy who didn't lead a very exciting life. Maybe if I told him about the time I was on this very highway years ago with three of my friends after a few beers in a borrowed Lincoln Continental, all of us too young to drive, let alone drink. Or the scrapes we'd sometimes get into with some of the guys from the other schools. Or other things we liked to do for fun. Getting older has all kinds of hazards. Forgetting to tell what you've *really* been up to in your life just might be one of them.

Todd looks back on his life fondly. That much is evident on practically every page of "The Life of a 1970s Teenager." But he doesn't see it all through rose-coloured glasses. Emotions aside, Todd is a realist. While these stories are told with affection, they chronicle his actual life, which contain moments of hurt, failure, and struggle. It would be easy for this narrative to simply be a feel-good road trip back to the 1970s – playing vinyl records, driving muscle cars, and wearing bell bottom pants. Those details are included, of course, but they are included for a purpose; not as a Hollywood backdrop but to bring the reader inside the circle of a person's life.

Sometimes the anecdotes unfold like the reader is experiencing them firsthand, with innocence, curiosity and humour. Whether it's avoiding the police, playing sports, or hanging out with friends, there is a free-wheeling spontaneity in these passages. At other times, there is a sense of serious retrospection. Early on, he watches his parents with a kind of reverence – as they work, socialize and raise their family; somewhere he intuitively understands that there is something heavy and complex in their lives as adults. Fast forward to later parts in the book and you see the twenty-something Todd facing challenges: trying to find a suitable career, raising children, and putting up with the sometimes hurtful commentary of family and friends as he tries to make things work.

Aside from all the nuance, if there is one constant in this book, it is the beguiling character of Swansea, the small former village in west end Toronto where these stories are set. Even in a world of gentrification, up-scaled homes and nowhere-but-up house prices, this book makes it easy to part the curtains of time, and find yourself standing in the Bueler's 1970s-era living room. Those who know Swansea will agree that its streets, laneways, fields and ponds haven't changed much through the decades. The Bueler family home, at 85 Lavinia Ave, is still there, and it's not difficult to imagine the children inside back then, watching *Captain Kangaroo* or *The Friendly Giant* on TV.

Around the corner, the Rennie Park of today is still essentially the same place described in the book. The park is a hub for hockey, sitting on picnic benches, and all manner of youthful pursuits. Up the hill, at Swansea School, even if students now have cellphones and are dressed in 21st century styles, Todd and his buddies would easily recognize that old building. The hallways have the same trophy cases and banners, and there's not much you can do to change the decor of the classrooms.

In some ways, Swansea is a part of the city that time forgot. Whether in the chill of winter, or the heat of summer, those signature streets are still alive with the universal themes of youthful rebellion, happy and tough times with friends, dating, dream cars, music, and coming of age.

Though most of this book is set in a small neighbourhood in a big city 45 to 50 years ago, it is not bound by geography or time, or targeted at one type of reader. The operative word in the title is "Life." Anyone who has ever lived one will be able to relate to the content of the following pages. Ultimately, what makes it all relevant and readable is that Todd has done what every memoirist should do: tell the truth.

Chris Higgins, December, 2024

Author Preface

I have led a very eclectic life, but my teenage years in a small neighbourhood in Toronto called Swansea, in the 1970s stand out the most. No cell phones, no internet, no computers; and most of the time, no parents or adults around. We were on our own in our own little world, and we made the best of what we had together as teenagers. In the end though, I was just a boy, in a world I thought was my own to make. I couldn't have been more wrong.

It was a glorious time to be a teenager. There was no other time like it, and I would have it no other way. It was a time of incredible freedom, and we used that unprecedented freedom to do what we wanted, when we wanted, oftentimes with no consequences. It was quite a ride.

There is very little on the internet or in book form that shows what it was like to be a teenager in the 1970s. And nothing of what it was like to be a teenager in Swansea. I felt I could create that with this book, giving a unique personal perspective that people can connect to and enjoy reading.

When I read a short story or a book, I want hardship, I want conflict, and I want triumph that comes from adversity. I want excitement, action, and suspense. I want honesty, credibility, and authenticity; it has to be personal, and the sentiment needs to be clear. I want the protagonist to win in the end. I believe I have been able to do all of that for the reader, taking the same emotional journey I was experiencing, while giving insight into what it was really like to be a teenager in the 1970s.

The book is about what I did, what I saw, what happened to me during that time of incredible change, and how it all affected me, my future, and those around me.

The book is about personal, social, and cultural change. It's about my personal growth, the changes I went through in life, and the changes I witnessed and was part of. It's about how I tried to cut my way through the teenage landscape of the 1970s.

It's about the people I met, the situations I found myself in, and how I dealt with those situations.

The book is about love, loss, sacrifice, and struggle. Trying to live a moral life, and having the courage of your convictions, knowing when to walk away from a situation, and when to stay and fight. About how to find the right thing to do with little information, while learning from your mistakes. It's about seeking the truth in a world of often conflicting values – both external and the emotional struggles inside. It's about when to listen to others and take their advice, and when to make your own path.

Todd Bueler Swansea, Toronto. Summer, 2024

The Life of a 1970s Teenager

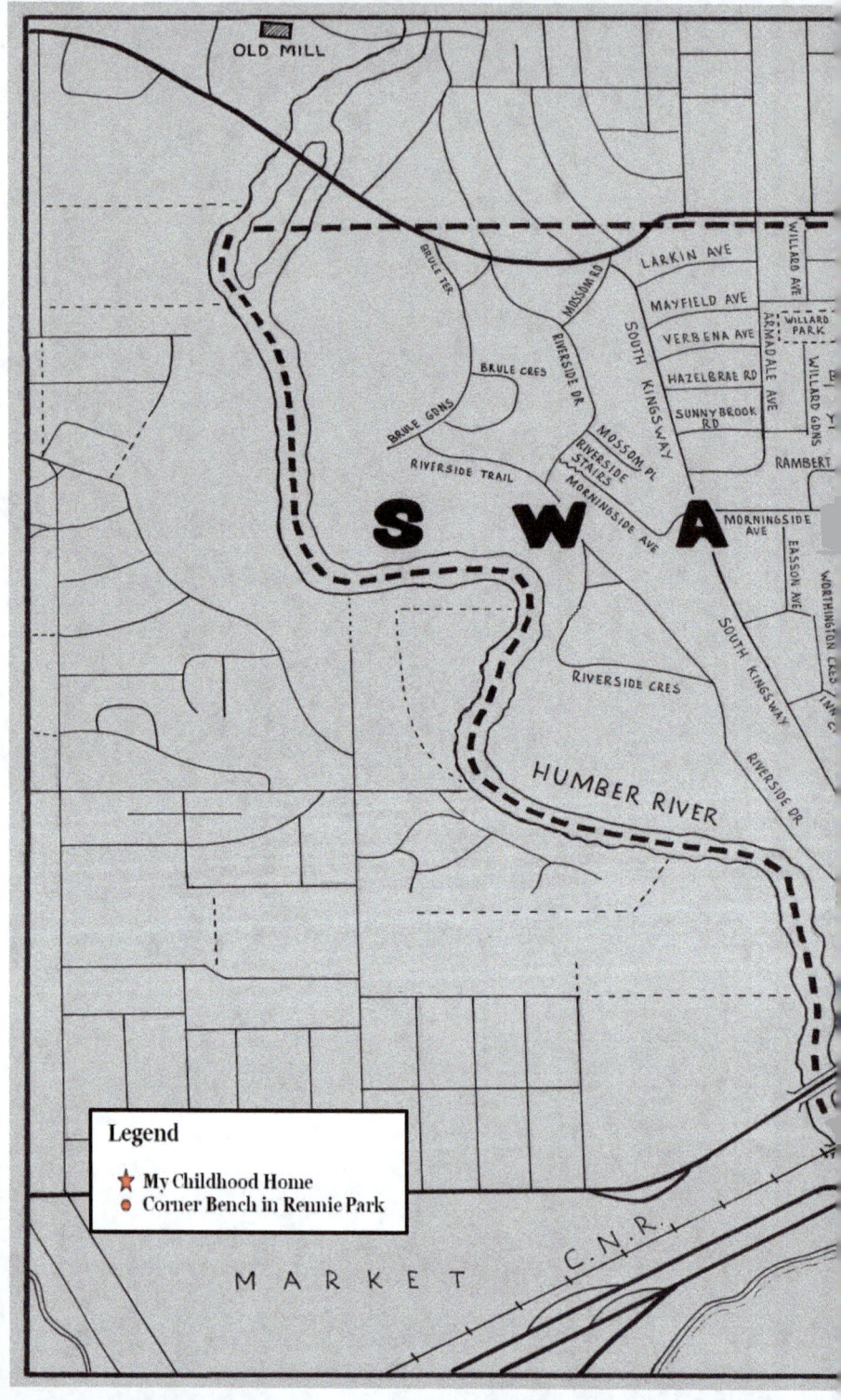

France:
Fairest Cordelia, that art most rich, being poor;
Most choice, forsaken; and most loved, despised.
Thee and thy virtues here I seize upon.
  – **Shakespeare,** King Lear, Act 1, Scene 1.

Midway through the journey of our life I found
myself, lost in a dark wood. For I could not reach
the path forward.
  – **Dante,** The Divine Comedy, The Inferno, Canto 1.

Introduction

Earliest Memories and Moving to Swansea

The youngest of four boys, I was born at Toronto Grace Hospital in the heart of the city in the early fall of 1962. My parents were born in and grew up in Toronto and in the mid-1950s they bought their first house – a brand new home in Aurora, a suburb north of Toronto. I never lived in that first house, as by spring of 1962, only months before I was born, my family had moved to a house just down the street from their first house. The address was 1 Johnson Road. I lived in the new house until we moved to Swansea.

In my teens, I asked my father about the first house. He told me they paid about $18,000 for it and had a mortgage of $16,000. The mortgage payment was just over $100 per month and his salary at the time was $100 per week, double what all his friends were making at the time. Both my father and mother told me all their Toronto friends told them they were nuts and could never afford that high of a mortgage payment. I asked him if they ever told their friends about the kind of money he was making at the time to show them they could afford it easily. My father told me no, it was none of their business, and they would see soon enough that they could handle the house with no problem, which they did. It was a two-storey red brick house on a large corner lot in a brand new subdivision. It had three bedrooms and was about 1,800 square feet. I don't think the house is there any longer.

My father started his career at IBM sometime in the mid-1950s. By the time I was born, he had risen to Programming Supervisor. At the time, this would have been a highly paid, highly sought after, but rare and difficult job to get.

He was 34 years old and commuting every day to Toronto. My mother told me that they went through a lot of cars in those days; my father also sometimes worked part-time jobs in the city on weekends, adding even more miles to the already over-driven cars. The daily commute back then – 45 minutes to an hour one way – must have also put a physical strain on my father. Big giant cars, bad gas mileage, no power steering, no power brakes, and the heavy city traffic once he got to Toronto didn't make for a relaxing drive.

From the middle of Aurora into downtown Toronto is about a 32 mile commute one way. My father did that commute day in and day out every week, five days a week, and sometimes six days a week. That's about 310–370 miles per week. Every week, week in and week out. It must have been killer. My dad's favourite car that he ever had was a 1956 Ford Fairlane. But after years of heavy commuting from Aurora to Toronto in the late 50s, the car gave up the ghost. He loved that car, but the transmission and engine were starting to go, and he needed a reliable car to commute, so he had to sell it out of practicality.

I now empathize with my father so much about those times. Together with four children, a brand new house, a high-end demanding position so early in his life, and living the full new mid-century suburban lifestyle, it must have been a very stressful time.

I know that most people think that you can't have any memories from when you're younger than four years old, but I have two memories that my mother confirmed for me when I was an adult. I have read some studies that confirm you can in fact have memories from when you're as young as two years old, so I believe that the small memories of my very young life are real.

I remember being at a house with my mother and being under a kitchen table playing, while my mother visited a friend of hers.

Introduction - Earliest Memories and Moving to Swansea

I remember my mother's friend spoke loudly, almost yelling, and that she was a little overweight. I asked my mother if she ever had a friend who looked and spoke like that. She told me yes, but it was in Aurora, and she hadn't seen her since our family moved to Swansea when I was two.

Another memory I have is of my dad bringing my brother and me bowls of cereal in front of the TV in the living room of the Aurora house. I asked my mother about this as well. She told me that there were times when we lived in Aurora that she worked weekends as a private nurse and my dad took care of us at those times. So again, this memory seems to be real.

In 1964, when I was two years old, my parents moved the family to a house in Toronto. The house was on a quiet residential street in the middle of a small neighbourhood called Swansea, in southwest Toronto, close to Lake Ontario. Our house was at 85 Lavinia Avenue.

Right around this time, while my family still lived in Aurora, my maternal grandfather had died of cancer at St. Joseph's Hospital on The Queensway in Toronto, not far from the Lavinia house, and my grandmother was having a difficult time being on her own. My mother was doing her best to keep an eye on her at the time, but my grandmother had her ups and downs, with more downs than ups. With all the driving back and forth from Aurora to the city, and my mother not being able to see my grandmother as much as she needed to, it finally got to the point that my mother felt that she needed to live closer. When she told my father she believed they should sell the house in Aurora and move the whole family into my grandmother's house in Swansea, he was not too happy. My father didn't want to uproot his family and leave his house after being comfortable there for years, and just after getting into the swing of things in the prime of his life.

After many arguments and discussions, my father, being the good man that he was, a man who loved my mother, relented and agreed to move to Swansea. It was a huge sacrifice that my father was making, but in the end, he felt he had no choice.

I asked him many years later to tell me a little about life in Aurora. He told me that at the time, he and my mother had embraced the new suburban lifestyle and any possible suburban stereotype. He worked like crazy, helped with the kids when he had the time, and did all the things people did in the suburbs of the late 1950s and early 1960s.

He would wash the car in the driveway on Saturdays, have big parties at the house in winter with all their new friends, and hold big back yard barbecues in the summers.

There were kids running all over the place, with the men in khaki pants and short sleeves standing around the barbecue drinking beer from cans. The women made salads and lemonade, laughing together while yelling at the kids, and lovingly joked with their husbands to not burn the steaks. I have a short snapshot memory of being in the back yard during one of the barbecues and seeing my dad young and thin, cooking on the grill with a huge smile on his face. He loved his family, his house, and his job. My father told me it was the happiest time of his life. He was 36 when we left Aurora.

The land where 85 Lavinia Avenue would be built was purchased by my grandfather in the mid-1940s. Over the course of the next two years, he built the house that is now still there and moved his family in around 1946 or 1947. He was an auto mechanic and later became an aircraft engine mechanic, working on the now famous Avro Arrow interceptor aircraft. He built and worked on the Arrow's turbojet engines at Malton Airport, which later became Toronto Pearson International Airport. There was a two-car, two-storey concrete cinder block garage in the back of the house that had a mechanic's pit, where my grandfather would fix the neighbourhood cars in the 1950s. My mother lived in the house until she married my father in 1949 when she was 18 and my father was 21.

My parents had four children; the first was born in 1954, the next in 1957, the third in 1960, and finally I was born in 1962. My father's name was Arthur and my mother's name is Joyce.

Introduction - Earliest Memories and Moving to Swansea

When the decision was made to move, a small self-contained apartment was built in the basement of the house for my grandmother to live in and the family would live on the upper two floors of the house. The house wasn't big, about 1,500 square feet or a little smaller. There were two bedrooms upstairs and my parents turned the dining room on the main floor into their bedroom. The two older kids were in the front upstairs room while my other brother and I took the back bedroom. It wasn't the best arrangement for two adults and four young boys, as the house was much smaller than the house in Aurora, and it was tight. But it wasn't much different than other houses and families in the neighbourhood.

With all that done, we began our new life in Swansea. Since the day we moved into the house (except for a short stint in south Etobicoke), I have lived in Swansea my whole life, and I still live there today.

It is important to note as you read through the book, a lot of the stories inside may sound incredible, even fantastical. To that I will say; ya know, it's been an interesting life growing up in Swansea. To live your whole life in a 10 block radius may seem odd to some, but it's all I've ever known. You tend to get more involved in things than if you moved around a lot. There are a lot more little nooks and crannies to life as you get more intimate and familiar with your surroundings. I had been thinking about all of this one day as I was writing and an old saying came to mind: "The truth can not only be stranger than fiction, but often, less believable." Truer words have never been spoken. Every word in this book is true, it all happened, and I'm happy to have the opportunity to share these experiences.

Now that that's out of the way, let's jump in, back to the 1970s. I hope you enjoy reading it as much as I enjoyed living it. The past is not dead; it lives inside each and every one of us. Now, turn the page, and together we'll enter the world, and the mind, of a 1970s teenager.

First Memories
Of Swansea

I have very few memories of when I first moved to Swansea. I was only two years old, and my memories of Swansea don't start until around age four, before kindergarten. Those memories are of going on walks with my mother and having a few friends visit to play and watch TV in the mornings. I remember watching *The Friendly Giant, Davey and Goliath*, and *Romper Room* on television.

I do have a memory of a particular moment while on a walk with my mother. We were walking through the Swansea schoolyard on a brisk, chilly morning; it was quiet and peaceful. There was no one else around and no wind. We walked to the top of the hill overlooking the school field and stopped. You could see the big old house over on Ellis Avenue that was probably a quarter mile away or more. There were no leaves on the trees to block the view, so it must have been late October or early November 1966.

As we stood there looking for a short time, I started talking. I don't remember the exact content of the conversation, but at the end of it I asked her, "Does that mean that as each day passes, we are all getting closer to when we die?" It was not those exact words I said, but it was something to that effect.

You would think she would have looked at me strangely for asking such an existential question as a four year-old boy. She did not. She looked east, out across the open field and without looking at me, she answered in a very nonchalant way, "Yes, but it's okay. That's a long, long time away from now." Then she reached down and took my hand. She looked at me and asked, "Does that bother you?"

"No, I was just asking." And we continued our nice, slow little walk through the schoolyard.

For some strange reason, this memory and many of the details are still clear in my mind as if it happened only yesterday. Throughout my whole life, it comes back to me often. I don't know why. Could it be it was the first time I thought about my own mortality?

Ya Little Puke

In the hockey season of 1969/1970, I played defence for Supertest in the Swansea Hockey House League. Supertest was a gas station on the corner of The Queensway and Park Lawn Road who sponsored our team. I was seven years old, and it was my first year of hockey. Two years prior, my mother had taken me skating at Rennie Park rink. I saw the older boys playing hockey and I told my mother I wanted to do that, and she said maybe next year. I wasn't fazed and thought, okay, but it ended up being two more years before I got to play.

Not at the start, but my first few years of playing, I would put my skates on at home, and then walk through the laneway behind my house, up Durie Street, then down Morningside Avenue to the park. I either had skate guards on, or I would walk on the tips of the blades. When I got tired from walking on the tips, I would walk on the full blade. When I got to the park, if there was ice, or if the grass had frozen over, I would skate through the park to the rink.

There wasn't enough room in the downstairs rink level locker rooms for both the young kids and the older kids, so the little hockey guys, the five, six, seven, and maybe even eight-year-olds, had to use the upstairs clubhouse to get their skates on. I hated changing in the upstairs clubhouse; it was always so crowded with people who were pleasure skating getting their skates on, and parents and volunteers helping the little fellas put on their skates and equipment. That was why I put my skates on at home. I stopped doing that later on when I got older, after I had access to the locker rooms at rink level before a game. I don't know how often I did it, but I remember doing it.

So, I put my skates and equipment on and hit the ice for my first year of hockey. Even though I was little, and skated on my ankles, I skated with all the enthusiasm I could muster. Every Saturday when I came home, I told my family we won the game. This went on for the whole season. One day, when I came home, my older brother Mike said, "You need to stop lying. You didn't win every game." I just shrugged my shoulders. I didn't care what he said, it was true, the team won every single game that year and we went on to win the championship.

I remember the game where I scored my first goal ever and my only goal that year. It wasn't what you would call a good goal, but it was an important one. Near the end of the game, I found myself inside the other team's blue line, and I had the puck! I took the shot and to my surprise, the puck went past a bunch of players and slid between the goalie's legs. I scored! Yay! It was the only goal of the game, and we won 1 to 0. I remember there was a lot of head shaking, but it didn't bother me.

When the time came for the banquet, where they give out all the trophies for the year, the whole team lined up to get our championship trophy. The trophy was small, but I didn't mind. When I got mine, it was the biggest deal in the world to me and I held it tight as I walked back to our table.

When we were all seated back at our table, one of my teammates, an older kid whose name I can't remember, looked at me and said, "Bueler, you don't deserve that trophy. You did nothing to win it, ya little puke." I looked back at him and said, "I scored the winning goal, not you." I wasn't hurt or upset or anything.

When I left the recreation centre on Lavinia Avenue that day, I walked home clutching my trophy with my head held high. I made a difference that year. I scored the winning goal.

The Neptune Factor

It was the summer of 1973, and I was 10 years old. One hot day that summer – I can't remember many summer days in the 1970s when it wasn't hot – Mr. Gerry Masters, a father of six and a Toronto police officer, who lived up the street from my house on Lavinia Avenue, ran out to the back of his house to his money tree. He grabbed a bunch of cash, and then took me and a bunch of other kids to downtown Toronto to see a movie.

We parked near the south end of Yonge Street, and we all walked up to the Imperial Six Theatre not far from Dundas Street. Yonge was blocked off to traffic south of Richmond Street, so it was a huge pedestrian walkway with open cafés and people sitting at tables which were in the middle of the road. That was something I had never seen before.

We walked out of the blazing sun and heat and into the ice cold, air-conditioned theatre. We got our tickets and ran over to line up at the snack bar. Mr. Masters bought us all cokes, chocolate bars, and popcorn. After getting our food, shoving each other around, spilling our popcorn, and calling one another stupid names, we ran into one of the six theatres, and tromping down the aisles, we noisily took our seats.

We saw a movie called *The Neptune Factor*; the story scared the heck out of me, but it was great.

Mr. Masters must have had some crazy patience. I think there were five kids with him, but I never saw him get mad at all. We all were bouncing off the walls the whole time. I hope he knows what a great day he gave me. I'll never forget it.

I'm Down Here!

In the early to mid-1970s, I remember the summers were very, very hot in Swansea. We didn't have air conditioning in our house on Lavinia Avenue, so my mom would set up the big metal floor fan and put big bowls of ice cubes in front of it to try to cool us kids off. Many nights, we would sleep downstairs in the living room as it was too hot to sleep in our bedrooms upstairs.

During those hot summer months of my youth, my friends and I would go swimming almost every single day. We went to either the High Park pool which always had freezing cold water no matter how hot it was outside, or the huge Sunnyside pool, which had a very high diving board. I always hated having to run through the ice-cold showers before entering the pool area.

We would swim all day long. When the pool closed for lunch, we would buy a hot dog to eat with a Coke while we waited for the pool to open back up. I had a dark tan during those summers and my eyes were always bloodshot from all the chlorine in the water. I never got sunburn, just a very deep tan. When I did get sunburn, it was hard to tell, as it was a deep brown with a red tinge.

Of course, during our trips back and forth to the pools, we would always have some type of adventure. Heck, I even saw the queen one day in High Park as she rode by in her gilded carriage doing the old royal hand wave!

One day in the summer of 1973 when I was 10 years old, I was on my way home from High Park pool with my friend.

I'll call him Stevie. Stevie, who had flaming red hair, was a little distance in front of me as we walked down a big hill in the park leading to Ellis Park Road which is a street on the west side of High Park. At one point, I had to stop to pick up my swimsuit that had been rolled up in my now unravelled towel and I yelled for Stevie to wait up for me. I heard his muffled yelling, but as I continued walking down the hill, I couldn't see him anywhere.

As I got farther down the hill and called his name again, I heard him yell, "I'm down here!" I could hear him, but I couldn't see him, so I kept walking down the steep path, looking around and calling his name. When I was about three quarters of the way down the hill, I saw him! Well, not all of him; all I could see was his mop of red hair and his shoulders sticking up from the path. We all wore medium-length shaggy hair in those days and his hair stuck out like a sore thumb against the brilliant green of the trees.

Somehow, he had fallen into a deep hole a little to the left of the middle of the path. We hadn't seen the hole earlier in the day as we had walked along Bloor Street to get to the pool, plus, we hadn't been to High Park pool for almost a week going to Sunnyside instead.

I walked up to him and started laughing. I said, "Holy crap, man! Are you okay?"

"Yeah," he said, "but I can't get out."

What the heck happened?"

"I was walking down the path and just fell into this hole."

"Didn't you see it?"

"Well, no, or I wouldn't be in here, would I?"

I laughed again, reached down, and pulled him up enough for him to climb out of the hole. He had cuts all over his arms and legs and a big bruise on one of his legs. We looked down into the hole and it was at least three feet deep. Someone had dug that hole and covered it up with grass and twigs. We moved all the shrubbery away from the hole so it could be seen from the path and continued the walk home with Stevie limping all the way.

When we went back a few days later, we saw the hole had been filled in. After that day, we were always extra cautious walking up and down the path. We never did see any more holes.

I Warned You!

Almost every Saturday in the 70s, I played Swansea house league hockey at Rennie Park from ages seven through thirteen. It was very cold most days, and I remember having freezing cold fingers and toes. I always thought I had frostbite.

Players didn't play in every game since there were many teams in the league, and during those times, we would watch the games from behind the rink fence with some of the parents. One day when I was 10 or 11, while I was not playing, I was watching the game and Jimmy Smith and Adam Jones were on the ice. I can't remember, but I'm almost sure Adam was playing goalie and Jimmy was playing centre on the opposing team. Both of their fathers were behind the fence watching, and Mr. Jones kept yelling at Jimmy and calling him a bum. Jimmy was very good – a Wayne Gretzky-type player. He was not big, but he was a good stick handler who scored a lot.

Mr. Smith kept telling Mr. Jones to stop calling his son a bum, but he didn't listen. I think you can see where this is going. I was about five feet away from them, and as the situation was getting more heated, I stepped farther away from them both, but I paid close attention and kept my eye on them.

Mr. Jones was ignoring Mr. Smith's warnings and continuing to call Jimmy a bum just after he scored again. Mr. Smith had had enough of the name-calling and walked up to Mr. Jones. He cold cocked him right in the nose, and Mr. Jones went down. Blood started pouring out of his nose like crazy; it looked like a garden hose of blood – it was everywhere.

I Warned You!

Mr. Smith simply said, "I warned you!" and then just walked away. Mr. Jones got up, blood all over him, and he just walked away too.

I was in total shock and had stepped back even farther after the punch. Nothing similar ever happened after that between them that I know of, and I don't think anything ever came of the incident.

Pro tip: Don't repeatedly call the son of a man who is right next to you a bum.

House Party on Lavinia

I was around hippie-type people in my early youth. Not often, and not for long, but I remember being around them.

I was 10 years old, it was the summer of 1973, and one evening I walked into a house party on Lavinia, it was a Saturday night about 8 p.m.

The house is still there; it was just south of the crest of the Lavinia hill on the east side. There were about 15 people in the house and I remember a girl, Lori McGregor. She must have been at least five years older than me. I remember her distinctly from her freckles and lazy eye. I was in the house and she found me in the kitchen with some other people about her age. I remember the strong smell of marijuana along with Jimi Hendrix music playing, I had no idea what the smell or the music was at the time. Someone handed me a can of beer and I opened it and started to drink from it when Lori appeared out of nowhere and took it from me.

There was some kind of kerfuffle as Lori fought with the others about her taking the beer from me. I didn't understand at the time what they were talking about, but I wanted to drink the beer. I was grabbed by a girl and pulled away from Lori and she gave me her beer to drink from.

Lori walked right up to the girl and said, "What's the matter with you? He's only a boy." Then Lori took my hand, smacked the beer from it, and grabbed my arm as she pulled me out of the house. She took me out to the sidewalk and said, "This place is not for you." Then she told me to go home, right away!

I turned and went home. I walked the short distance to my house and with only one or two exceptions seeing her on the street, I never saw Lori again.

Lori did the right thing that day. I was too young to be there with those older teenagers, and of course drinking alcohol at 10 years of age, was not something that any boy should be exposed to. Lori had the foresight to remove me from a situation that I was way too young to understand and should never have been involved in in the first place.

The Poke Check Kid

In the winter of 1973/1974, when I was 11 years old, I played for Runnymede Hardware in the Swansea Hockey House League on Saturdays. I was a defenceman, and I did my job well.

The winters were very cold in the 70s, with this winter being about the coldest I can remember; freezing temperatures every single day with snow nearly as often. After each game on those cold days at the outdoor rink at Rennie Park, I felt like my toes had frostbite as I walked home. My house on Lavinia Avenue was heated with radiators, and there was one in the living room right beside the TV. It was so nice being home, and straight away after taking my coat off, I would lie on the floor and stick my feet in between the radiator spokes. My mom would make me a Fluffernutter sandwich – Marshmallow Fluff spread and peanut butter on fresh, super sweet white bread with a big glass of strawberry milk. I would sit in front of the TV while eating and drinking, and watch wrestling or minor league hockey on CHCH TV channel 11 from Hamilton. There was no cable TV then; all we had was an antenna and a black and white TV. I didn't care, though. I was warm, relaxed, and had nothing to do. I was enjoying my post-hockey afternoon.

In the middle of the season, on a cold January day, we had a late morning game. With a few minutes left in the third period, our team was ahead by one goal.

I had gotten a penalty, and as I was released from the penalty box, an opposing player crossed the centre line with the puck, on a breakaway towards our goal. I skated as fast as I could to catch him, but he was too far ahead of me. At the last second, when he was about 15 feet from our goal, I gave a few last strong skate strokes, and using my momentum, I dropped down on my stomach and slid across the ice, my stick out in front of me. About 5 feet from our goal, I poke checked him from the side, knocking the puck off his stick, denying him the shot.

My check changed the game from a tie to a win for my team. I was one of the last kids off the ice, and when I walked into the locker room, someone yelled out, "Here comes the Poke Check Kid!" All my teammates let out a huge cheer as I stood in the doorway and they soon all began chanting, "Poke Check Kid! Poke Check Kid!" I felt pretty good.

This became my signature move, earning me the title of Poke Check Kid amongst my teammates.

The season ended and it was now time for the hockey banquet, where they gave out all the trophies and awards for the year. Unfortunately, I became sick with the flu, and was too sick to go to the banquet. I was heartbroken that I couldn't be there to have fun with all my friends, but I had to stay home.

Late on that cold Saturday afternoon, as I was lying on the couch watching the wrestling stars Sweet Daddy Siki and The Sheik on TV, there was a knock at the front door of my house. My mom answered the door, and after some muted talk, she said it was for me.

I got up from the couch in my cowboy pyjamas and saw my coach standing in the doorway. He told me he knew I was sick and was sorry I wasn't able to attend the hockey banquet, the whole time holding his right hand behind his back. Then, bringing his hand around in front of him, he revealed two items: a trophy and a single hot dog wrapped in aluminum foil.

He handed me the trophy, and I stared at the etching on the plaque; my name and the words "TEAM MVP" glittered in the afternoon sun. I broke down into uncontrollable blubbering; though I did have a tough exterior, I was a bit of an emotional kid at times. I thanked my coach through my tears and waved back as he left. I don't remember the coach's name, but I'll never forget his face and I'll never forget what he did. He made a sick young boy very happy that day.

Riverside Drive
And the Big Rec Room

Riverside Drive was where the wealthy kids lived, but most of them still went to Swansea School with the rest of us. Riverside is on the western border of the neighbourhood between South Kingsway and the Humber River. Riverside was a separate place, a micro neighbourhood inside a neighbourhood, if you will, and the kids from the main central grid section of Swansea didn't go there much. There wasn't a big separation of class; it wasn't like that then from what I can remember. It was more of a distance thing. All the recreational stuff – Rennie Park, the Swansea Recreation Centre, and the school were in the main neighbourhood grid. There was simply more to do there. Some of us would go to Riverside on occasion to visit friends from school in their large, beautiful homes, and I was up there a few times while I was in grade school. However, I'll never forget the first time I went.

It was the winter of 1973/1974; I was 11 years old and in grade six. Kelly Fisher and I were in the same class, and one Friday, Kelly invited me to come over to her house on Riverside the next day, to have lunch and to stay the afternoon. Kelly was a girl; of course I said yes, I'd be there. In my head I was thinking, *With bells on!*

I didn't have a hockey game every Saturday; sometimes we had the day off, and this was one of those days. Even if I did play hockey that morning, if it was cold, I never hung around the rink after a game, so my afternoons were free.

Kelly's house was at the far southwest boundary of Swansea at the bottom of the hill on Riverside Crescent. I lived in the main grid of the neighbourhood, and Riverside was a world away in my kid mind. It was at least a 20-minute walk, probably longer, from my house on Lavinia Avenue no matter which way I went. It was a long walk, made longer by the cold, the wind, and the blowing snow. I took the shortest route down the steep Morningside Avenue hill west of Windermere Avenue, to South Kingsway at the bottom. I walked up the hidden Riverside stairs at the end of Morningside after crossing over South Kingsway, up to the Riverside escarpment. Then I started the long walk from the north on Riverside Drive to the stairs at the south end of Lucy Maud Montgomery Park that would take me down to Riverside Crescent and Kelly's house, which was at the south end of the street.

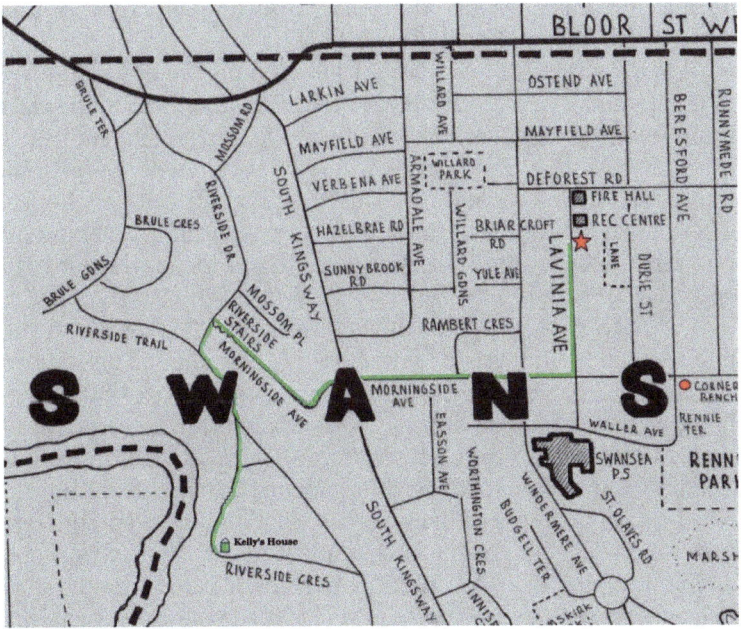

Map of the route I took to Kelly's house that cold day in the winter of 1974. Red Star is my house.

The Life of a 1970s Teenager

I remember Swansea winters in the 70s as the coldest of my life, and this winter was no exception. When I got to Riverside and turned left to walk to Kelly's house, the sun became covered in clouds and it got dark. Shortly after the top of the stairs, there is a sharp left turn going south. As I rounded the corner, the wind coming from the south started to pick up. As it howled and whipped all around me, I heard what I thought was thunder in the distance. The snow wasn't letting up and it was starting to freeze. I had to lean forward and walk with my head down to stop the tiny ice pellets from hitting my face. Sometimes, just to be able to keep going, I had to turn around and walk backwards as the cold wind was too much. Even though I wore thick wool socks and heavy winter boots, I could feel my toes starting to get cold. I didn't see a single car on the street, and the only sound during my journey was the wind whistling all around and through the trees as I passed by the big houses.

When I got to Kelly's house, I knocked on the door, and her mom opened it with Kelly beside her. Stepping inside, the first thing I noticed was that the house was big, warm, and spotlessly clean. It was also quiet, since the only people who were there were Kelly, her mom, and me. This was different from my house, where I had both my parents and three older brothers, meaning I was rarely alone, and it wasn't quiet often. I took a deep breath and relaxed.

I went to a lot of friends' houses in those days, mostly in the main grid. Sometimes for a few short minutes, other times for an afternoon. What is embedded deep into my mind is that everything was old in those houses. Besides the interior decor, it all seemed like a black and white photo – grey. What little colour did exist was muted. Kitchens, basements, garages, front porches, back porches, soggy back yard lawns, and cracked concrete driveways – all old. Some basements had dirt floors. On cool, damp spring or fall days, the musty smell like that of a cottage was ever present, as were a lot of things made of wood, including stairs, floors, porches, shelves, and doors.

Home renovation was a rare thing then, so most houses in Swansea were pretty much the same as they had been when they were built 50, 75, or 100 years earlier. It all felt so inviting, warm, and welcoming.

This house was different, not that it wasn't those things. I can't remember if it was new, but it wasn't like anything I was used to.

Kelly's mom looked at me after I took my coat off and said, "My goodness, son, you're shivering. Come sit by the fire and I'll make you kids some lunch." Her name was Claire, I told her thank you, and Kelly and I went to sit down. We sat by the fire in the middle of the living room, and I warmed up right away. There were two big picture windows at the side and end of the living room, overlooking the snow-covered back yard. This was something I had never seen before; it was so beautiful, and I couldn't stop looking outside.

Kelly and I sat and talked about school for a bit, a little gossip about our classmates, and some funny things that had happened during the past week. Then she asked me, "Was it really cold walking to get here?"

I told her, "It was, but it's nice and warm here." A short time later, Kelly's mom brought us some warm, buttery, toasted salmon sandwiches, two bowls of tomato soup, and big glasses of cold whole milk. This was a treat; we didn't drink whole milk often at my house, it was too expensive. We had 2% milk, and I could tell how much more I liked the whole milk.

I was warm now, and very hungry. Everything tasted so good.

After lunch, Kelly and I went downstairs to their rec room. This room also had large picture windows that looked out to the back yard, and there was another fireplace there with a nice, warm roaring fire. Two fireplaces in one house? I felt like a very lucky boy that day.

This room was big – bigger than I had ever seen in a house. I was only 11 years old, so my perspective then may have made the room seem larger. We played cards, board games, listened to music on a 45 record player, and sometimes we sat and talked. I don't remember watching any TV.

Kelly's mom popped in occasionally and asked if we were hungry or if we wanted something to drink. We had hot chocolate, strawberry milk, potato chips, orange pop, and possibly cake throughout the afternoon. I don't remember everything she brought us, but we seemed to be eating and drinking the whole time I was there. This was not unusual for me. As a kid, I was constantly eating and drinking no matter where I was, as were my friends. The thing about being a kid in Swansea in the 70s was, you walked everywhere. In the summer you could bike, but in the winter you walked. Parents never drove you anywhere. If you wanted to go visit a friend, no matter how far it was, you were on your own, and this made for a big appetite.

The afternoon passed quickly, and I wasn't paying attention to the time when a passing glance at the clock showed 4:30. I was having so much fun with Kelly I didn't want the day to end. Kelly's mom called downstairs to Kelly to say it was time for her friend to go home. Kelly yelled back up, "A little longer, Mom!"

"Ten more minutes. It's going to be dinner soon," came the reply.

When more than 10 minutes had passed since Kelly's mom had called down to us, I told Kelly I thought I should be going. She said okay, but then something happened – we started kissing. I don't know how, but I know why, and I liked it. Kelly was super cute, I liked her, and she was a good kisser; I remember that one thing clearly.

Just then, Kelly's mom appeared out of nowhere; we didn't even hear her come down the stairs. Did she see us kissing? If she did, I thought I'd be in big trouble! I don't think I'll ever know for sure, but if she did see us, she didn't say anything right then. I'm guessing, judging by my interactions with her that day, and how nice she had been throughout my visit, that even if she did see us kissing, she was kind enough to not embarrass us both.

As I left on that overcast afternoon for the long, cold walk home, Kelly's mom gave me the sweetest smile goodbye. It was a different smile from what she had given me when I first arrived at the house. It made me think she knew what we'd been doing. She also told me to come back soon, and that I was welcome in her home anytime. You can tell a lot from a simple smile.

I don't remember ever speaking with Kelly about what had happened. In the end, it was a fun first experience I had up on Riverside Drive, and I enjoyed myself.

Kelly and I never did become an item – the story of my young romantic life, I guess. It was something that happened that I liked, and that was it. Many times, I look back on those days and say to myself, *I was such a fool. What was I thinking?* I should have pursued Kelly then, but like so many other girls I liked, I was too immature to see what could have been, and I left it alone.

If Kelly ever happens to read this, and she still remembers that day, maybe one day she can let me know how I did with the kissing bit.

The Tom Trilogy

A Game of Muckers

Tom and Nick – not their real names – were about two years older than me. If anyone from the neighbourhood remembers or heard about this incident, you'll know who Tom and Nick are. If you're a little squeamish, you may want to read this story with a little warning.

One day in the summer of 1973 or 1974, I was at the Rennie Park rink playing a game called Muckers with a few friends. I think the game's real name is Quoits; it's like Horseshoes, but you play it with rubber rings instead of metal horseshoes.

The Muckers pit was at the bottom of the stairs that led from the upper level park clubhouse to the lower level hockey and lacrosse locker rooms, and the entrances to the two rinks. There was a paved path between the bottom of the stairs and the Muckers pit. Beside the stairs were some trees and some bushes.

There was a small pick-up game of lacrosse with a few fellas being played on the big rink at the time, and you could watch it from behind the rink fence. If you were watching the game, you could turn around and in a few steps be in the Muckers pit. The pit ran north to south and about 20–25 feet in length, and the rink ran west to east.

It was summer and hot, so we were all wearing shorts and t-shirts. There were four of us playing Muckers, two at each end of the pit, and one guy watching the lacrosse game. That guy was Nick. I was at the north end of the pit, and the stairs were at the south end.

In the middle of our game, Tom silently appears out of the bushes at the south end of the pit, and stands there for a second or two. We all look at him, except Nick, who's had his back to us watching the lacrosse game. Tom puts his left index finger to his lips to shush us, even though we said nothing. Then, out of nowhere, he produces a dart in his right hand, shows it to us, and grins. We stop playing our game and there is just silence. I think you can guess what's about to happen.

Tom raises his right hand and aims the dart. Then he throws the dart and it's a perfect shot, even though thrown from about 10 feet away. It hits Nick right in the middle of his right thigh, but below his shorts.

Nick lets out a yelp, but no scream. There is still complete silence, except for the sound of Nick's moaning. He has his arms up and against the fence holding on and looking over his shoulder at his thigh. There is a small trickle of blood running down his leg and the dart is sticking out. This all happened in under a minute, but it felt like five.

Tom slowly walks across the pit and to the right of Nick. We're all stunned but can't look away. He gets very close and speaks into Nick's right ear, "Want me to take it out?"

"Yes," Nick replies, but Tom doesn't take the dart out right away. He turns, looks at us, and shoves the dart further into Nick's leg, then pulls it out. This time, Nick let out a scream.

Tom turns around, walks back across the pit, and then up through the bushes where he came from, while giving us the most evil smile I can remember. There was something wrong with that guy Tom. He was just a dangerous person to be around.

This One's Hot

Once again we have a perpetrator and a victim in this story. Both were about two years older than me at the time. When I first wrote this story, I didn't remember the victim, but I had it narrowed down to two people. I have since confirmed the victim's real name. The perpetrator was Tom, the same guy from the previous story, A Game of Muckers. In this case, I'll call the victim Edward. There were a lot of people present when this story happened, so again if anyone from the neighbourhood remembers or heard about this incident, you'll know who Tom and Edward are. This story is not for the squeamish either.

On the north end of the old Swansea School building, sometime in the 1950s, I believe, an extension was built connected to the main school with a long hallway running south to north that had floor to ceiling windows spanning the length of the hallway. The hallway led to several new classrooms, an auditorium, and the kindergarten classrooms.

After you finished walking north through the windowed hallway, the first classrooms you came across were the woodshop on the right, and the home economics classroom on the left. Mr. Anderson was the woodshop teacher and Mrs. Miller taught Home Economics.

One day in 1973 or 1974, I was in shop class and I was in Grade 6. For some reason, there were some older guys in the class with me. I can't remember why, but there were a lot of people in the classroom that day; it was probably a combined class.

Everyone was milling about doing their own thing: cutting wood, sanding, painting, and drilling stuff. Mr. Anderson was walking around the class watching everyone, and helping out where needed.

I was sitting at a bench close to the door sanding a piece of wood. When you walked into the classroom, to the left against the west wall, there was a sink and a water fountain with a handle you would push down on to activate the drinking fountain.

I didn't know the reason at the time, but Tom was at the fountain calling guys over, asking them to take a drink and see if the water tasted funny. A few guys came over and said, "No thanks." It was a strange question for Tom to be asking and they might have known what was behind Tom's request, or at least knew it wasn't a good idea to be involved in anything Tom was doing.

Tom was a known troublemaker and very few kids trusted him. As I mentioned in my previous story about Tom, he was a dangerous guy to be around. If you saw him, you needed to keep your distance.

I overheard what was happening and I felt something was up, so I kept an eye on what was going on.

One kid, Edward, took Tom up on his request. I looked over and watched as Edward put his hand on the fountain handle to take a drink; it was a bad idea. The moment he touched the handle, he let out a huge yelp. I didn't know why, but for a few short seconds, his hand was stuck on the handle. He ripped his hand off and I could see some skin still on the handle.

By now, the whole class had stopped doing whatever they were doing and everyone was looking over at the fountain. Tom had stepped back, grinning. Mr. Anderson had come running over as Edward was holding up his hand. I could see Edward's palm was very red and obviously badly burned.

I later found out what Tom had done was put a small hand torch to the handle of the drinking fountain and held it there until the handle turned white hot. It cooled off quickly to the point that you couldn't see the change in colour of the handle, but it was still hot enough to burn someone. I never saw him do this, but I believe he did this over and over to keep the handle hot. He must have kept the torch hidden as he did it so no one could see him. That guy was a bad dude.

Championship Ping Pong

Once again, it was the summer of 1973 or 1974. I was at Rennie Park and had just walked into the clubhouse; the door was always wide open in the summertime. You could go into the clubhouse anytime and get sports equipment to play your desired game – like a Coochie ball, or some bats and gloves to play baseball. Only Swansea people would know the game of Coochie (see Appendix A).

I walked in to get a pop from the vending machine inside, and there was a ping pong table just inside the door. As soon as I walked in, I saw Tom and I stopped dead in my tracks. He saw me and said, "Bueler, ping pong?"

I said, "Sure, I'll play ya." Bad idea!

Now, I was pretty good at ping pong, and pool (billiards). I got to be good from countless hours of playing these games at the Swansea Recreation Centre on Lavinia Avenue.

As the game progresses, I start winning. I can see Tom is growing agitated, and I'm thinking I may have put myself into a not very good situation.

At this point, I am thinking about how I can get away fast. I notice I am close to the door and I can get out before Tom can reach me, if needed. Anyway, the game ends and I win.

Tom is pissed that I won. He has his own baseball glove with him, and he throws it at me. I duck, and the glove misses me. At this point, I know it's time to make my exit.

I run for the door. Just as I'm almost there, Tom whips the ping pong paddle at me – 3/4 inches of plywood. As usual, Tom is an excellent shot. The paddle hits the bottom of my left ankle as I'm almost out the door, and I go down. The pain is intense, and I fall out the door, rolling onto the concrete right outside the entrance.

I'm now down on the concrete moaning in pain, and I can't get up. No one comes out to see how I am, and I'm lying there in excruciating pain for a few minutes continuing to moan until I'm able to get up. All that time, I'm defenseless and in fear Tom will appear at the door to rain more pain down on me, but he doesn't come outside to finish me off.

The pain subsides, and I get up and start to limp away towards the west. I look in the window as I'm leaving the area, and I can see Tom is playing foosball at the other end of the clubhouse like nothing happened.

Tom almost broke my ankle, then just walked away to play another game without a thought about me, or what he did. I shook my head and limped my way home. My ankle was swollen for two days afterwards, and I was in pain and limping for three days.

After that, I never interacted with Tom ever again, and I don't know what became of him.

Swansea School Funnies
Grade 6

By the time me and my friends had gotten to Grade 6 at age 11, we were starting to test the limits of our teachers. It started in Grade 4, and one thing I remember doing from that year to disrupt the class, among other things, was to get clumps of plasticine from art class, and throw them at the blackboard as the teacher had her back to us writing on the board. The plasticine would land with a thud and stick to the blackboard. By the time the teacher had turned around to try to catch whoever it was who threw it, all she found was a class of giggling students. Before this, Grade 3 was quite different, all I remember about that year was learning more in-depth reading and writing, and for some reason I have almost no memory of Grade 5 at all.

By Grade 6 we no longer tried to hide our antics. The stuff we did was done right out in the open. Going to the office, getting detention? We didn't care in the least. Here are a few quick stories from that year that are still clear in my mind.

Part I

One day in 1973, our Grade 6 teacher, Mr. Ratcliffe, asked us to turn in our homework from the night before.

As Mr. Ratcliffe walked around the classroom gathering up the homework, he got to the table where I was sitting with some other students. Now, I have a friend who I'll call George, and we were always getting into some type of trouble together. When he asked George for his homework, he said he didn't have it. Mr. Ratcliffe asked him where it was and, without skipping a beat, George looked up from his desk and said, "It's still in the pencil."

There was stunned silence for about 15 seconds, probably less, as Mr. Ratcliffe and the rest of the class took this all in – it was a long 15 seconds. Then the whole room broke into uncontrollable laughter. After the laughter subsided, Mr. Ratcliffe looked down at George and calmly said one thing to him, "Go to the office, George."

I'll never forget that day or the brilliant response George gave to Mr. Ratcliffe.

Part II

Another fun story from my Grade 6 year at Swansea School starring my old school chum, George. One day close to Halloween, we were all coming back into the class from lunch. On this day, our teacher, Mr. Ratcliffe, was away, and we had a substitute teacher. We had had her before, so we knew her, and she knew us. Her name was Miss Zigamont, but out of her earshot we all called her Ziggy. The things we put her through that year were astounding. Looking back, I'm surprised she didn't have a nervous breakdown when we were done with her.

I had an idea George was going to do something as he entered the classroom, but I didn't know his exact plan. On a side note, I remember every little detail about this event like it was yesterday.

While we were in the hall before class started, George pulled out a rubber gorilla mask from his back pocket and showed it to me. Prior to this, I didn't even know he had it.

"What is that?" I asked him.

"It's a mask. What does it look like?"

"I know what it is. What are you going to do with it?"

"You're about to find out!"

About a third of the class was already inside and George told me to go in before him. When I asked him why, he said, "So you can see the whole thing."

"Are you sure you want to do this?" I asked.

"Just do it," he said with an evil grin. So I just shrugged and said okay. He put the mask on, and I walked into the class with George in the mask close behind me. When I was about three quarters of the way into the room, I saw Ziggy looking at us from the front of the classroom. George stopped about halfway in and turned to face the front of the class. He put his arms up, and out to his sides like a vaudevillian actor. Then while proceeding to shake his whole body, he yelled out, "ZIGGYYYYY!" in a muffled voice through the mask.

I was completely shocked as a huge smile came to my face and I looked up at Ziggy at the front of the room. The students in class were half looking at George and half looking at her. Unfazed, Ziggy raised her left arm, pointed to the door, and said, "Go to the office, George." The woman's patience was incredible.

For that little stunt, George received a week's detention. Later in the day, I asked him if it was worth it. He said, "For sure, what do you think?" and I told him, "Absolutely!"

Waking Up!
Detention Time

I do mention how I was a streetwise and intelligent kid in other stories, but not in a criminal way as the term is so often used. My upbringing was different from most. I was the youngest of four boys, and my parents weren't involved with me much. If I was home when I should be, and no cops ever came to the house, I was left alone. Plus, I had pretty much no respect for authority of any kind, except for my parents. I have left a lot of money on the table over the years in my work life for my refusal to capitulate to what others want to try to make me do.

I was not above speaking to adults in any fashion I wanted, and I did that often. I didn't care about any repercussions or suffering any consequences for my actions. Even though I would argue my point, I always knew that I may have to pay a price for reacting the way I did when I thought that a wrong was being done to me.

I can't say that for a lot of my classmates and friends at the time, though, but there were other kids in the neighbourhood who behaved like I did. This common behaviour made us gravitate towards each other and we became friends, but these kids were rare.

As a young boy, it was natural for me to always act and think in a critical manner, and to question everything all the time. I was like this from a very early age, and although I was contrary most of the time and rarely went along with what society thought

I should do, be, and how I should act, I didn't always know the reasoning behind the way I acted.

There were a few turning points in my life where I became aware of what I did, what I said, and the way I approached situations and people, made a difference in how my life was affected and how it affected those around me. It wasn't until around Grade 6 when I was 11 years old that this began to happen – I was waking up. After that, my resolve to stand up for myself grew stronger, and that was obvious in my actions, and in my ability to confidently speak my mind. I was always very aware I was different from most, and as I grew and matured, my personality development intensified along those same lines. Some would call this defiance, and upon reflection, I guess it was.

Here are a couple of short examples of my realizing what I did and said made a difference, and I had some type of control over what happened to me.

Writing Lines

When I was in Grade 6 at Swansea School in the 1973/1974 school year, I had gotten a detention, and I was made to write lines.

For those who don't know what "writing lines" is, it's a form of punishment usually done while in detention. You had to write the same sentence repeatedly for 50, 100, or more times on paper. The sentence would be about what you did wrong. An example would be, "I will not talk in class." This was used at times in elementary school during the 70s, though I don't think it is used anymore.

I wrote a couple of pages of lines, and my hand started to get sore, so I stopped writing. My teacher said, "Why did you stop writing? You're not finished."

I said, "My hand is sore. I am finished."

"You need to keep writing lines until you're done, or we'll stay here all night."

"I'm fine with that. But I'm not writing any more lines."

My teacher did not respond. Fifteen minutes later, he said the detention was over and l went home. I never wrote another line ever again. I was such a little devil.

Gym Class

The following year, 1974, when I was 12 and in Grade 7, was the first year of rotating classes. Prior to Grade 7, most subjects, like math, English, and history were taught in one room by one teacher. When you advanced to Grade 7, you would start the day by attending home room. After homeroom, you went to different classrooms with specialized teachers for each subject. Physical Education was one of those subjects.

The gym teacher assigned to my class had a reputation; let's just say, he liked to look at the boys. There had been rumours all over the school for years about this guy and his inappropriate attention towards boys. I took about three gym classes at the start of that year, and on those three occasions while I was changing out of my gym clothes, I noticed the teacher was looking at the students taking a shower in a mirror that was looking right into the common showers. I refused to take a shower after gym when I saw that. After the fourth class, the teacher told me if I didn't take a shower, then I didn't take gym, and I told him that was fine with me. He also told me I would have detention every day I did not take gym and I told him I was fine with that too!

I never took gym again, and would get detention every time, but I didn't care. One day, before this little showdown ended, he grabbed me by the arm and told me I was going to take gym as he tried to drag me into the locker room where all the other kids were getting changed for gym class. I pulled away and told him to "Fuck off," and if he ever touched me again, it would be the last thing he ever did – this was when I was 12 years old! He didn't know what to do or say at that point, and I stood there waiting for his response. After a moment's thought, he turned and walked away. He never tried to get me to take gym again after that day.

In the end, I went to about three detentions, and then I stopped going. After that I was told by the principal I would be spending the time for gym class in the library if I didn't want to take gym, but no more detention. And that was the end of that; it's what I did for the next two years during Grades 7 and 8. I sat out every gym class in the library with another schoolmate who chose to do the same as me.

Awake

After these events transpired, I had an epiphany and noticed I wasn't being watched all the time; in fact, almost never. People were so busy with their own lives trying to keep things together, so if it didn't involve them, most people couldn't care less about what anyone else did. I also noticed if I didn't want to do something, I simply didn't do it, and the adults never had much recourse. I was awake to what was happening around me.

During the course of writing this book, with all the childhood memories flooding back, I have been doing a lot of self-reflection about how I have chosen to live my life. Here's what I've learned, and how I have reacted to challenges that have been presented to me over the years.

Don't let people criticize your personal or professional life. People who criticize others in a non-constructive fashion are projecting their own inadequacies onto you. If anyone ever questions your professional abilities, or your personal integrity, state your credentials or your morals. Have confidence in your own abilities and life experiences. Doing so shuts down negative people, not doing so emboldens them. It can be done in a diplomatic way, and the more you do it, the easier and more natural it becomes.

Contentment

In addition to the above, here is a list of what I have found has brought contentment to my life. I have done my best to not waver from these points and I sleep better at night as a result.

- Don't do anything to jeopardize your personal integrity.
- Always think critically.
- Question everything.
- If you feel something is not right, trust those feelings.
- Always stand up for yourself.
- Take calculated risks as much as possible.
- Pick your battles. Not everything is your fight, nor is everything worth fighting over.
- Take responsibility for your mistakes. Admit to them, learn from them, and try not to repeat them. This will garner sincere respect from others, and will give you self-respect.
- Just because you can do something, doesn't mean you should.
- Have empathy for others.
- Don't let money be the driving force in your life. Doing so, you just may find it wasn't worth it after all.
- Don't live in anger or conflict.

Walk Out on Your Hands

One Saturday afternoon in the winter of 1974/1975, a few friends and I were in Pete's Restaurant on Bloor Street. For those of you who were never in Pete's, the restaurant was long and thin. It had 10 four-seater booths running down one side, each with red vinyl seats and mini jukeboxes, and counter service with swivel chairs half the length of the restaurant on the other side.

That day, we were in a booth at the back, and I was sitting facing the front. The restaurant did have a few other people in there then, but it was not busy at all. My older brother, Kim, who was eight years older than me, came in with some of his buddies. One of my friends said, "Oh shit! Bueler, it's your brother!" My brother never bullied me, but he would embarrass me and bug the heck out of me in front of my friends if he ever saw me in public.

I saw him, and I ducked down while he and his friends sat down in a booth near the front. My brother sat with his back to me, and he didn't see me. *Phew!* I thought, as I sat up and we all continued to fool around and act like idiots while we ate our fries with gravy and drank our Cokes.

I remember looking towards the front and occasionally watching my brother, to make sure he didn't turn around and see me. While I was looking at him, I noticed he had the broadest shoulders of anyone I knew. He was the only one on that side of the booth, and he was sitting in the middle of the seat. It looked like he took up the whole width of the booth.

At this time, the owner of the restaurant had a standing offer to his customers that was quite unique. If you could walk on your hands, down the few stairs and out the front door of the restaurant, he would give you $20. That was a lot of money back then.

I turned my attention away from my friends as I saw my brother get up from the booth. The owner came out from behind the counter with his dirty white apron on and a crisp $20 bill in his hand. My brother's friends also got out of the booth, but they didn't have their coats on, even though it was wintertime. I was wondering what was going on, but I think you can guess.

Right then, to my surprise, my brother bent over and tried to get on his hands. *Now* I knew what was going on. After a few unsuccessful attempts at this, he gave up. His buds patted him on the back, and no one laughed or anything. This was serious stuff.

Everyone went back to their seats, and that was it. Sorry for the abrupt end, but that's just the way it happened.

As an afterword to this story, I do remember one older teenager did do this successfully during that time; however, I never saw it, and I don't remember his name.

A Little Quick Money

One day in the summer of 1975, when I was 12, one of my buddies and I were walking down Beresford Avenue, just south of Deforest Road. A taxi cab passed us and stopped to drop off its passenger a few hundred feet ahead of us. When we were about 50 feet from the cab, we saw the driver retrieve some items from the trunk for his passenger. As he walked back to the driver's door, he dropped something in the middle of the road, got into the cab, and quickly drove away.

We couldn't see what it was that he had dropped until we got closer. To our surprise, it was a roll of cash consisting of $1, $2, and $5 bills amounting to about $45 or more – this was a lot of money for a couple of young boys at that time.

Instead of doing the right thing, we took the money and went to Dufferin Plaza, which was five subway stops from our neighbourhood. This was in the days before the plaza was enclosed and renamed Dufferin Mall. We spent the money like a couple of drunken sailors – no offence to any drunken sailors out there.

We bought food, stupid hats, t-shirts, pop, candy, pocket knives, and played a lot of pinball games. After a few hours, one of the store owners noticed we had pulled out a lot of cash from our pockets to pay for something. He asked us why we had so much money and where we got it from. That was enough for us to know it was time to go. We promptly ran away, left the plaza, and hopped onto the subway to go back home.

My buddy, for some reason, decided he would accumulate as much change as he could with his half of the money during our little excursion. Both of his front pants pockets were filled with change, and he jingled as he walked. When we got back to Swansea, we both made our way home. It was dinner time and after about an hour of me being home the phone rang; it was my buddy's mom.

The jig was up. After she spoke to my mom, my mom took the $10 I had left. My buddy also had what he had left taken from him by his mom, though all in change.

I can't remember what happened after that and I feel bad about it now. We should have done the right thing, but we didn't. I think I remember both of our parents tracked down the cab driver and returned what was left of the money, but I'm not sure.

All I can say is we were young and that was the most money we had ever had or seen in our lives. I believe we also felt since the money was from an adult, it wasn't that much for him. Of course, we were wrong on all points and any justification for taking the money for ourselves was misguided. We knew it wasn't our money, and keeping it was wrong. At the same time, we felt we weren't hurting anyone – a strange dichotomy for sure. We thought we were lucky to have found it. Such was the thinking of young boys back in the mid-70s.

It's strange how little incidents like these stick in your head for over 50 years.

The Greatest Gig

Music played a pretty big part in my life during my teenage years, and when I hear this song now, all I can think about is when I was young, and dirt poor. But we had a heck of a lot of good friends always around, and nothing but time on our hands. I guess I wasn't so poor after all.

When did I first hear this music that is so ethereal? Well, it was the late summer of 1975. I was just about to turn 13, and I was ready to enter my last year of elementary school. There was a party at the Masters' house up the street from my house on Lavinia Avenue, and there were no parents there.

I walked into the open house around dusk and there were a lot of older guys and girls there who I didn't know. Music was playing in the background and lots of people were talking. It seemed safe to say the older Masters' sisters were having a party. I was looking for either of the Masters' brothers, John or Bill, to hang out with, but neither of them was there.

Frank Masters, who was a few years older than me, was walking down the stairs as I was looking around. He saw me and said, "Hey, Bueler, come up to my room, I want you to hear something." We went upstairs and he showed me a record album with a prism on the cover. I had never seen it before.

I asked him what it was. He said, "It's Pink Floyd." Then he carefully took the album out of its sleeve, gently put it on the turntable, and slowly dropped the needle down onto that glorious piece of black vinyl. The first sound I heard was a heartbeat, then some strange talking, a clock ticking, the sound of a cash register, and eerie laughing. Before long, the music began to envelop me; it was something I had never experienced before. I was mesmerized. We sat in his room and listened to the whole first side of the album without speaking to each other. The needle on the turntable lifted off the album automatically, and the muffled sounds of the party downstairs now floated up to the second floor of the house replacing this strange new music. Without saying a word, he flipped the album over and the needle dropped for the second time. Then the sound of a cash register again, followed by a walking syncopated bass line. Again, this was a type of music I had never heard before, and I was struggling to understand it.

When the album was over, I couldn't speak for a few seconds. Frank asked me how I liked it. I had no answer, so I just said, "I don't know what to say."

Frank said, "Ya, I know."

I walked downstairs and went home in a sort of daze. I went up to Sam The Record Man on Bloor Street a few weeks later when I had the money and bought the album. I taped it onto a cassette using my brother's stereo and took it with me all over the place to play for my friends. After that day, music changed for me and started to become a much bigger part of my teenage years. I went from listening to bubblegum music – a sub-genre of Top 40 music – to more mature, serious, 70s rock, almost overnight.

In my teenage years, the crowd I ran with were, well, pretty tribal. Looking back now, we were very into ourselves, to the point of, if you didn't get our music, you were on the outside, and we were on the inside. If you didn't listen to our music, you were Not Cool! As a teenager in the 70s, being cool was a big part of life. You could be ostracized, if you didn't listen to our music.

Those of us "on the inside," were aware of our pretentiousness, and we didn't care. As an adult now, I realize how ridiculous and immature it all was then. But at the time, it was important.

You could come into our fold if you were into our music – to a point. There were other ways of getting into our group besides music – having a "not give a crap attitude" got you in. We would sometimes put aside what we didn't like about you – whatever that might be – if you knew, liked, and understood our music, but not always. You were judged on your musical preferences a lot of the time, and sometimes you were even talked about behind your back based on that.

Some of the music we listened to was, for the most part, mainstream. But most of it was on the fringes; that was how we kept our clique exclusive. Bands like Supertramp, Styx, Boston, The Beatles, Led Zeppelin, Van Halen, Pink Floyd, and Rush were more mainstream. Then we had progressive rock bands like Genesis, U.K., Yes, Gentle Giant, Emerson Lake & Palmer, King Crimson, and Strawbs.

The world of a teenager in Swansea in the 1970s was an encapsulated entity of its own, and music was a big part of that. When my daughter was in her 20s, we would joke about it by saying, "This... is serious music!" I still listen to it all today. To tell you the truth, I still have a little pretentiousness about the music, but the difference now is, I don't care whether others like my music or not. I guess you can't ever leave your past behind.

This was also the time of "The Lane," a small, grass-covered laneway/walkway between two houses, more like a footpath, that runs east to west off of Lavinia Avenue. It's a few doors south of Morningside Avenue, about 100 feet from Swansea School. It connects to a laneway at its west end that runs south to north between Waller and Morningside that you can drive through to reach garages belonging to the homes on Windermere and Lavinia.

In Grades 7 and 8, when I was 12 and 13, this was the place where I would hang out before and after school with some other miscreants, and at lunchtime, we would smoke cigarettes and enjoy each other's company. This was an exclusive club and if you weren't invited to "The Lane," you didn't come there; this point was understood throughout the neighbourhood. There were about 10 of us altogether, split between guys and girls. Anyone who tried to infiltrate "The Lane" was given the cold shoulder until they left. It didn't take long for them to come to the understanding that they weren't wanted!

We were the Rockers, looked upon as the Burnouts. But in reality, we were just a bunch of kids trying to make our way like everyone else. We took the false labels as a badge of honour and let it ride. No one screwed with us as we were thought of as toughs. I know it's odd to think of 12 and 13 year olds as toughs, but that's the way it was, and we embraced it and laughed about it all the time. We were outsiders and kept to our little group of friends. We let the others think what they wanted; we couldn't have cared less.

A Weekend at
The Swansea Rec Centre

The following events occurred over the course of one weekend in the early spring of 1976. I had turned 13 the previous September and was in my last year of elementary school.

I was coming into my teenage years and started to be a little more, how should I put it, experimental, a renegade, independent? Of course, I wasn't the only teenager in the neighbourhood doing the same thing.

It's all fairly tame, but fair warning, it's a little, well... one or all of the adjectives above.

In the Swansea of the 70s, most teenage kids had little adult supervision, unless there was an organized event. At the time, Swansea was much more of a working-class neighbourhood than it is today. Most parents either didn't have the time, or didn't mind too much about where their kids were or what their kids were doing outside of the home. Not all parents, but almost all the kids I knew had parents like that. There were many reasons for this, such as money issues, work problems, stress. Also, it was a more laid-back time to bring up kids in general. There weren't as many real dangers for kids as there are now. Of course, if something bad happened, a rare occurrence, the parents paid attention.

This was a time with no cellphones, no internet, and no computers. Most houses had one phone and no extensions, and no telephone answering machines. Few houses had air conditioning, so no one wanted to stay inside during the summer; it was too hot. There was a lot more freedom from adults in those days, in my life anyway. As I wrote earlier, if you didn't come home in a cop car, or too late at night, it was all good.

Being able to leave the house at almost any time I wanted was the norm when I was growing up. There were times when I couldn't do that, but almost never. On those rare occasions, there was sometimes a little pushback from me, but in the end, I had to stay in.

I never talked back to my parents or disrespected them in any way; they were the adults I listened to and respected. When they told me to do something, I pretty much did it. My parents never hit me. Punishment in my house was being grounded, either for the evening or possibly a few days. For me, that was much worse than being hit. Not being able to see my friends for any length of time was devastating for me, and I remember it would cause me a lot of anxiety. Since I was never hit, it's difficult to say what effect that would have had on me compared to being grounded. Being grounded did leave a big impression on me and I tried hard to avoid it.

Part I – Friday Evening

Moonshine, Vodka, the Cops, and the Dance

For me, the weekend started out just like any other at that time in Swansea. School was done for the week, and the phone calls had started to come in for planning what we were going to do that Friday night. There was lots of yelling from my mom and dad about getting off the phone when the calls lasted more than five minutes, as I either made or received call after call from my friends. The weekly Friday night dance at the Swansea Recreation Centre was in the plan, as always. After the phone calls, the plans continued with showering and picking out the coolest clothes to wear for the night.

The dance didn't start until 7 p.m., but we were too anxious to get out of the house to wait. Our group included me and about five or six other girls and guys. We all met up at the top of the hill at the western dead end of Deforest Road overlooking Willard Park. It was about 6:30 p.m. and just starting to get dark. There is a little path that runs south to north from the top of that hill to Mayfield Avenue. That path had, and still has, a few trees that hid it from view from the park as it's elevated about 30 or 40 feet above it. We moved farther down the path to stay under cover and hidden from view.

We took our smokes out of our Levi's jean jackets and lit up as we talked over one another about the events of the week. We were all excited to be out on our own for the night. Everyone was talking a mile a minute while telling each other to shut up and pushing each other around. I remember everyone being very physical with each other in those days. There was a lot of shoving, smacking, kicking, tripping, and other shenanigans, and not just amongst the guys. Then my bud James pulled out a Mason jar from inside his jacket that was filled to the top with a clear liquid.

"What the heck is that?" I said.

"You know what it is, Bueler. I told you on the phone that I'd gotten it."

"I thought you were fooling around!"

James' dad made moonshine in his garage, not a lot, but enough for James to be able to take some and not have it noticed. One of the girls saw it and said, "Don't drink that, I heard you could go blind."

"Don't be stupid, my old man made it. It's fine. I've had some before," James said.

James handed me the jar and I opened the lid and smelled it, but it had no smell. "It's just water," I said, laughing.

"Take a drink," James said.

I took a sip; it wasn't water, and it wasn't bad. It was strong, and tasted like black licorice. James grabbed the jar and took a big swig, then handed it to Ben, who also took a big drink. The girls were all saying, "You guys are stupid," but we didn't care, and so we continued to take turns drinking the candy-flavoured moonshine.

We had almost finished the jar between the three of us guys when one of the girls, Suzie, who also happened to be my girlfriend at that time, pulled out a small bottle of vodka from under her coat. We were just about feeling the effects of the moonshine when she said, "Want some real booze, guys?" I shook my head no, as did James and Ben. She then pulled out a plastic bottle half-filled with orange juice and poured a lot of the vodka into it before shaking it up a bit. She shrugged her shoulders, took a drink, and handed the bottle to the other girls.

The girls passed the bottle back and forth a bit, and then us guys took a few more drinks out of James' jar as we kept bugging each other about whatever we could. A little bit of time elapsed and we finished off the moonshine, then about a half hour later the vodka was almost finished, and we were all drunk by that point.

It was dark and about 7:30 p.m. Just then, we saw a cop car with its lights off. It was creeping up from the south below us and into the cul-de-sac of Willard Park. Someone must have heard us being loud and possibly had seen us drinking, but the cops couldn't have caught us if they tried; we were too far away. They probably didn't even see us. It was time to go to the dance!

While heading to the dance, Suzie and I walked with our arms around each other. As we all staggered the three short blocks to the Rec Centre, laughing and shoving one another, one of the girls, Jane, tripped and fell to the ground. She was right in the middle of the street laughing and rolling around on the road. As she laid on the ground at the top of Deforest Road and Windermere Avenue, a fast-driving car came around the corner headed straight for her. Suzie took her arm off me, ran into the street, and pulled her friend up and off the road just in time. The car came to a screeching halt and the driver yelled out the window, "What is wrong with you kids?" We said sorry and he drove off shaking his head.

We made it to the north end of Lavinia Avenue and continued to walk the short distance to the Rec Centre. As we walked down the front stairs to go through the door, I turned around and saw a cop car as it drove slowly by, heading north. My eyes met the eyes of the cop in the passenger seat as they passed. He pointed at me as I let the door close behind me. We were safe inside the Rec Centre.

We walked through the lobby and into the huge rectangular room straight ahead where the Friday and Saturday night dances were always held. There were a lot of kids there, maybe 30 or more. Seventies pop music was playing, and the lights were low. We headed in and took up the northeast corner of the room. As time went by, there were a few dances, a draw to win the latest 45 record, and some chips and pop. We were all laughing and yelling at the person doing the draw. A couple of our other friends came over and said, "Ha! You guys are all drunk." They were right; we were all drunk and laughing, having a great time.

Soon, the lights went down and a slow song came on, so Suzie and I got up to dance.

As the song was ending, I saw Ben and Jane get up and walk out of the room. Suzie broke off the dance with me, curious to see what they were up to. I went back to the corner and James told me he thought they both went to the bathroom.

"At the same time?" I asked.

"Yup, I think they're sick."

Oh great, now we're in shit, I thought to myself.

Before long, Suzie appeared at the entrance to the big dance room and motioned me over to her.

"Jane's drunk and throwing up in the bathroom," she said.

"No kidding, what about Ben?" I asked.

"He's in the guys' bathroom throwing up; I think you should go in."

I went in to ask him if he was okay. He looked up at me, pale white, and said, "I am now!"

I headed back to the dance, and a bit later, Suzie came and said she was taking Jane home, and then going home herself.

Ben had already left too. I was ready to go with her, but she said no, so we kissed goodnight and went our separate ways.

Soon James and I decided to go home too.

"See ya tomorrow, man," James said.

"See ya!" I said, and walked the short distance to my house in the now quiet darkness.

When I was almost to my house, I saw a cop car just over the hill, coming north towards me. I kept walking, and as I went into the house, I saw it pass.

I turned my head around and said, "Good night." My mom was in the front room and had heard me. She asked me who I was talking to.

"Just talking to myself."

"Are you okay?"

"Ya, g'night, Mom."

I went upstairs to my room and fell asleep. The night was over, but the weekend had just begun.

Part II – Saturday

My Mom's Car, More Cops, and a Narc

I wake up late on Saturday morning at about 10:00 a.m. and the house is empty. At that time, my mother had just won the Canadian Doubles Esquire Roller Skating Championship. She was training in preparation for the world championship competition and her skating partner would pick her up early to go to practice. My dad was at work, and I don't know where my brothers were.

Downstairs a little later, there's a knock at the door and it's James from the night before.

"What's going on, Bueler? Feelin' okay?"

"I'm fine, what about you?"

"Those guys were real babies last night."

"Yeah," I say.

"So whaddya wanna do, man?"

I look down at the table near the door and see the small bowl where my parents would leave their car keys. I pick up the keys to my mom's car and say, "Let's go for a ride."

"Cool!" says James.

We walk out of the house, look around, get in the car, and take off down Lavinia Avenue. The car was a blue 1971 Toyota four-door automatic, with a four-cylinder engine.

We drive around Swansea, not too slow, but not speeding. This is my second or third time driving, so I am cautious and paying super close attention to everything around me. There is little traffic. After driving around for a little less than an hour, we see some people we know and they start yelling, "Bueler's driving! Bueler's driving!" *Thanks a lot*, I think. We both just smile and wave.

After driving around a bit more, we start driving south on Beresford Avenue towards Rennie Park. When we're almost at Morningside Avenue, I look in the rearview mirror and a cop car is driving slowly behind us, just cresting the hill. I don't know if he's seen us, but I'm not taking any chances and quickly pull into a driveway at the bottom of the hill. I pull far into the driveway to the back of the house where the car can't be seen from the street. I shut the car off and listen. The only sound is our hearts pounding a mile a minute. We hear the cop car coming to a stop with its brakes squeaking – they may be looking for us! It's possible they think we're hiding, but we're not sure. Maybe they think they missed us and that we made a right turn going up Morningside.

We sit for a bit, and we know the cops aren't moving – we can still hear their radio. This goes on for what feels like a long time. James says we should just bolt through the back yards and leave the car. I tell him we should wait until we hear them coming up the driveway, and if they knew where we were, they would already be back here now. I don't think they know we're here, and we don't even know if they're looking for us. James says no, he's going now. "Just wait," I whisper to him, pulling him back as he quietly closes the door, "I don't want to leave the car unless it's absolutely necessary."

A Weekend at the Swansea Rec Centre

The cops haven't left; they are still parked on the street. Then, just as quickly as it started, it ends. The cops rev their engine; pop on the siren, pull a quick right turn, and bolt up Morningside hill going west.

"I told you to wait," I say. Everything is quiet again.

We wait a few more minutes, and then I start the car, back out of the driveway, and make a right turn to go up Morningside hill. A few feet before I make the right onto Durie Street, I see another cop car in the rearview mirror coming west down the hill on Morningside, and he's almost at Runnymede Road. I'm not sure if he saw me, but I put the pedal to the floor and race down Durie, pushing the Toyota's sewing machine-sized engine to its 25 mph limit, ha! With the little engine making a high-pitched whining that I'm sure the whole neighbourhood can hear, I make it to the lane on the left leading to my back yard garage behind my house. I catch what I think is a glimpse of the yellow police car turning onto the top of the hill at Morningside and Durie towards us.

I hit the gas again hard and the car's rear end spins a bit as I enter the lane, kicking up some gravel and dust and making it look like the tires are smoking. I look over at James and he's holding on for dear life as he's forced against the passenger door. My garage door is open, and I pull the car into the driveway and right up into the garage.

We jump out of the car, close the garage door, and sit down on the lawn chairs on the grass. To calm our nerves, we light up a couple of smokes.

Before long, we hear the squeaking brakes of the cop car coming up the back lane; they stop right in front of my driveway. My back driveway is about 50 feet long, from the lane to the garage. Two cops get out of the car – one is young and the other is older. The older cop motions for me to come down to the entrance of the driveway. Both James and I get up out of our lawn chairs and walk down the driveway.

The younger cop begins the dialogue and asks what's in the garage.

"My brother's '67 Camaro. He's rebuilding the engine," I say.

"Can we see it?"

"Sorry, it's locked, and I don't have the key."

"Well, we want to look in that garage."

"Why do you want to look in the garage?"

"We got a report that a couple of kids have been driving around."

"Not us."

Both cops step back and whisper to each other.

"Were you two kids driving a car around here earlier?" asks the younger cop.

"Who, us? No sir, we were just relaxing in the sun back here."

"Well, we know it was you, we saw you, so just tell us and everything will be okay."

"Officer, we have been here all morning. I'm too young to drive. You must have seen someone else."

"Yeah, right," he says.

"Look, boys," the older cop chimes in, "we know it was you, and if we ever catch you, you're both gonna be in trouble, so don't do it again." He then points at me and says, "I've seen you before; I'm watching you."

As they drive away, we go back up the driveway and open the garage door, light up a few smokes, take back our spots in the lawn chairs, and laugh about the whole thing. When we finish our smokes, we park the car back where it was on the street. I put the keys back in the bowl, and then I'm outside again, walking up the stairs from my house to the street and talking to James about what we're going to do next.

Just then, a car pulls up and my mom gets out of her friend's car.

"Hi Mom, how was practice?" I ask.

"It was fine. What are you kids doing hanging around in front of the house?"

"Oh, we were just talking about what we're gonna do this afternoon. I think we're gonna go to the Rec Centre."

"Okay, be home for dinner."

"All right, see ya, Mom."

It's just past noon and the Rec Centre is open. We walk down Lavinia to the Rec Centre and go upstairs to the second floor into the games room, which is located on the south side of the building. There are a few kids in there playing pool, ping pong, and some are playing cards at the card tables. There's 70s pop music playing over the speakers and it's a mild, sunny day – not too hot.

There is a row of chairs on the north wall of the room opposite the pool table. We sit down and wait for our turn to play a few games of pool and then some ping pong. When we've played about half a game of pool, a kid comes into the room and tells me that Barry, the Rec Centre superintendent, wants to see me in his office.

"What for?" I ask.

"I don't know, but he says to come now."

I put away my pool cue, walk down the hall into the little lobby outside of Barry's office, and find the door closed. I knock and then open it about halfway, sticking my head into the office. Barry is sitting behind his desk facing the door, while chain-smoking menthols. There is another older kid in a chair on the left side of the desk.

"What's up?" I say.

"Have a seat," Barry says as he gets up from his desk and walks over to me. He flashes a police badge, then tells me to put my hands out in front of me.

"What for?" I say, standing up. I didn't put my hands out in front of me, but he pulls my hands towards him and slaps a set of cuffs on me.

"What the hell? Take these things off me. I've done nothing wrong."

"Relax, Todd, I just want to ask you some questions."

I sit down and look over at the other kid, and I notice he has cuffs on too. Barry then tells me he's a police officer and he's investigating drug dealing at the Rec Centre. I look over at the other kid while pointing back to Barry with my thumb and say, "This guy's a narc?" He just shakes his head.

Now, I was pretty contrary and somewhat combative when it came to adults at this age, and I had no respect for any type of authority. I was not scared at all, but I was starting to get angry.

"I don't care what you're doing or who or what you're investigating. Take these cuffs off me now and let me go," I say.

Barry ignores me and starts his interrogation by asking if I am dealing drugs, or if I know of anyone who is dealing drugs, all while continuing to smoke. I watch puzzled, as Barry is holding the smoke in his lungs from the cigarettes for a long time before blowing it out; I find it odd, it's interfering with my thoughts, and I'm having some difficulty paying attention to what is going on as he does.

Distracted from the chain-smoking, causing me to pause before answering I say, "Fuck off, and no. I don't deal drugs and I don't know anyone who does. Now take these fucking cuffs off me. I'm going home."

He was a little shocked at how I spoke to him, but he got up, took the cuffs off both of us, and told us we were free to go.

"This is a bunch of bullshit!" I say.

"I'll be watching you two!" Barry says.

As we are leaving his office, I tell him I'm going to tell my parents what just happened and he'd better watch it.

The other kid and I immediately left the Rec Centre. When I went back the next day, Barry wasn't there, and he never came back. I never saw or heard of him ever again.

Part III – Sunday

A Morning Punch and an Afternoon Slap

Violence in Swansea was a rare thing in the 70s, but it did happen on occasion. When it happened, it was short, fast, unpredictable, and it ended almost instantly. But there was a little violence on this Sunday.

I woke up Sunday morning to the smell of bacon. On Sundays, my mom always made a big, traditional breakfast for everyone, which included bacon, eggs, toast with jam, cereal, and tea. My dad was at work. This was normal for him; he worked a lot when I was a kid, so it was my three brothers and my mom at home, but my brothers never bothered with me much.

I went downstairs and my mom gave me a big plate of food. I plopped myself down in front of the TV and watched while I ate. I should have been doing homework after eating, but I decided to read the Sunday newspaper instead. It was ordinary for me to not do any homework in Grade 8. I did attend school every day the previous week, which was out of the ordinary for me. As the year went on, I started skipping more and more.

On Sunday mornings, the Rec Centre was half open. The upstairs games room didn't open until the afternoon which meant upstairs activities didn't start until the afternoon, but the basement opened at 9:30 a.m., so activities that took place there started early. The basement had a smooth, poured concrete floor; we used it as a mini hockey rink. This floor was divided in half, length-wise. One side had hockey nets at each end for floor hockey, which was played with what could be called broomsticks and a sort of cloth ring for a puck. The other type of floor hockey was called Cosmo. This game was played with plastic multicoloured hockey sticks and either a white hollow plastic ball with holes in it about the size of a softball, or a hollow orange plastic puck the same size as a regular ice hockey puck.

The other side of the floor had benches against the east wall, and was used for various games like badminton, and smaller games of floor hockey, and we did gymnastics there using floor mats and a gymnastics horse.

After breakfast, I went to the Rec Centre and got there just before 9:30 a.m. I waited with a few other kids on the front steps for it to open, and then me and five other kids followed the supervisor down into the basement to play some Cosmo.

The Rec Centre was a little strange in design, it was built on a hill, and five storeys tall, but only three floors. The main floor was two storeys tall, the top floor was one storey tall, and the basement was two storeys tall.

We followed the supervisor down the two big flights of concrete stairs to the basement. The stairs were long and steep with one turn at the landing. The individual stairs themselves were short, so you had to pay close attention.

Then we walked down the long corridor and entered the rink area. There were five of us there at that time, so we got the best pick of the plastic hockey sticks from the storage room. Since there were so few of us, we played a few half games while we waited for more kids to show up. About a half hour later, we had enough kids for a good full game – two goalies and four players on each side. We used the orange plastic puck that, if you got hit with it, would sting. Everyone heard it when you got hit; it was a loud ping sound, and boy, did it hurt. It also always left a red mark.

One of the kids who was playing net for the other team was a year older than us, an only child, and always had a chip on his shoulder. His name was Cameron, and he thought everyone had it out for him, which wasn't true.

I played centre or left wing, and I was pretty good. I could make that puck fly hard and fast. If one of my shots hit you, you knew it. I was scoring on Cameron a lot, but he was also stopping a lot of my hard shots. He had no goalie equipment, so when he got hit, he got hit hard.

About halfway through the game, I was hitting Cameron quite a bit. You could see red welts on his arms and legs from the puck. He was starting to get pissed at me, and it got to the point that he would throw the puck back at me whenever I scored on him or he took a particularly hard shot to his chest.

My next shot was one too many for Cameron. I had taken the shot from just beyond the centre line, which wasn't far for the size of the rink. It hit him square on the thigh with a loud smack! He bent over for a second, and then came after me. I ran back to behind my net while telling him to calm down. He kept coming, so I started to run around the little rink, down the sidelines and behind the nets. He was yelling at me, calling me all sorts of names, while all the other guys were yelling at him to shut up and get back to the game.

He was bigger than me but he was a little chubby. I knew I could outrun him no problem, but I was getting tired of the bullshit. After this went on for about three or four trips around the rink, I stopped short in front of his net. As Cameron came towards me, I warned him to stop, while I made a fist with my right hand and raised it to show him. But he kept coming. So when he got within striking distance, I cold-cocked him right in the jaw. He went down fast. I stood over him saying, "I told you to stop."

He was out cold for about 10 seconds, maybe more. My hand was pretty hurt. The supervisor came running over and said, "Go home, Todd."

"What about him?" I said.

"Don't worry about him, he'll be fine. Now go home."

"Yeah, but it wasn't my fault, and I told him to stop, but he wouldn't. You saw what happened."

"I saw what happened. Go home."

I turned to leave, mumbling under my breath, "What an asshole," meaning Cameron. A couple of my buddies patted me on the back, saying he had it coming and to not worry about it. I wasn't worried in the slightest.

I walked home, had lunch, and watched some old time wrestling on TV while I ate. I was going to go back to the Rec Centre when it re-opened at one o'clock, and I hoped the cops wouldn't show up and that I wasn't suspended from the Centre for a while. Whether Cameron would come back, well, that remained to be seen. But if he did show up and started up with me again, the result would be the same.

I got there a little later. When I walked in, I ran right up the stairs to the games room on the top floor. "Anyone see Cameron?" I said. He hadn't been there, but I kept my eyes peeled the whole afternoon anyway; he never showed.

The next few times I saw Cameron, I didn't say anything to him, and he never said anything to me. It wasn't discussed again. But I also made sure to not play any type of game with him ever again either.

A little later that afternoon, me and a few other guys were sitting on the wall-length benches against the north wall in the games room behind the pool table. While waiting to play a game, Top 40 music was playing through the stereo system again and we were watching other kids playing ping pong and shuffleboard. Across the room against the south wall, two card tables were full with kids playing various card games. I noticed at one of the card tables, there was some kind of commotion, but it was very quiet.

One of the guys at the table was Greg; he was two years older than us, but he was small and short, though not above fighting if he felt it was necessary. He was a little mouthy too, too mouthy for his size, and a lot of the time for no reason. Pat, Big John, and one other guy were at the table too. Big John got his name being the biggest kid around. He was 6'2" if he was an inch, and 210 pounds. John was a nice guy, but you didn't mess with him; he had a long fuse, but when he blew, stepping away was the best option.

Our pool game came up. A friend of mine racked the balls and started to play. There was still some commotion at the card table, something about not playing or not showing cards. It was getting a little loud, and I made a point to not get too close to them.

A few minutes passed, and I was at the far north end of the pool table, away from the card table. I was bent over lining up a shot, and as I was looking down the pool table, John got up a little from his seat and reached over the table and slapped Greg across his face, hard enough that it could be heard throughout the games room over all the noise.

I stood up, a bit surprised – even a little startled. Greg put his hand to his face and I could see a big red handprint on his cheek; it looked like a tattoo of John's handprint. Then John said, "Is that enough for you now?" Greg stayed seated and spoke not one word. John looked over at Pat and told him, "I'm leaving, you comin'?"

As John was walking out, Pat got up and followed John out of the games room. Everyone in the games room stopped what they were doing, stunned, waiting to see what Greg was going to do. But he did nothing. He just sat in his chair rubbing his red cheek. I walked up to him and asked him if he was alright. He told me to fuck off. That was good enough for me. I went back to my game of pool. Greg sat at the table for a few more minutes, then got up and left. We continued playing pool for the rest of the afternoon and the others continued with their games. The day ended and I never heard the issue brought up again.

I went home at four o'clock, watched a little TV, had dinner, and then went to my room to read.

I'd had quite an eventful weekend. As I laid my tired head down to sleep, I wondered, *Should I go to school tomorrow?*

Summertime Hijinks

This story comes from a conversation I had with Valerie, a dear friend of mine from the old Swansea days. We were boyfriend and girlfriend for a short time when we were in grade school together, and she's also in a later story in the book. We're still close and we talk and see each other often. We reminisce a lot, and during the beginning of my writing this book, she asked me if I had written about that summer night back in 1976.

I asked her what night was that? She started to tell the story and I stopped her after the first few sentences. I had forgotten all about it, but almost as soon as she started talking, it all came back to me. Well, most of it. This is the story of that summer night long ago.

It was near the end of August 1976. I was about to turn 14 in less than a month, and enter my first year of high school. The end of summer was near, and it was my last year as a real kid. When I was in Grade 8, my friends and I had ruled the roost, but soon I would be back at the bottom of the pecking order in high school. High school? *No problem*, I thought. I'll walk in there and show 'em what's what. There were still a few weeks left before the new school year started, so I wasn't thinking much about school. I had been top dog in Grades 7 and 8, and had no reason to believe that I couldn't saunter into high school with the same confidence and swagger as when I walked out of elementary school a few short months earlier.

I had a few older friends already in high school, so I wasn't worried about being a Niner. Plus, I had two older brothers who were well known in the neighbourhood and had a reputation at Western Technical Commercial High School. No one was going to shove me into a locker. No one would dare give me a hard time. I already had an undeserved reputation as a tough guy with tough friends, and with two older brothers who would think nothing of beating the crap out of anyone who would give me any guff, it wasn't going to happen. As it turned out, there never were any incidents, as I hardly attended classes anyway.

It was a crazy hot summer that year and by the third week of August it was well into the mid-80s°F. My close friends and I were on our own with little to no adult/parental supervision. Not even the cops bugged us much. But we had each other as we tried to find our way through that awkward teenage summer.

What we did to help with our teenage boredom that summer was, at times, outlandish. We never hurt anyone; we weren't like that. But we wanted, and badly needed, fun and excitement. Our appetite for those two things was endless. And the only way to get that was to make our own. And we did it every chance we got!

By this time in my life, I was growing up fast, and though I was starting to feel different, I didn't understand what was happening to me. I didn't know it at the time, but things were changing for me mentally, on a personal level. I felt it, but I couldn't control myself. Adolescence had hit, and I was a real teenager.

My fantastic, perfect, 70s early adolescent days were beginning to wane though, almost as quickly as they had begun. Gone were the days when me and my friends would spend Sunday afternoons at the old Terrace Roller Rink on Mutual Street in downtown Toronto to skate and try to meet girls, or sometimes at the Mimico rink in west Toronto.

The Mimicombo rink had a wooden skate floor, the perfect skating surface for doing the Whip.

The Whip was when you would get four, five, or if you could muster it, 10 people together. You would join hands in single file, and then start to skate around the rink, picking up speed as you went along. If you were at or near the end of the line, you would be whipped out of the line from the centrifugal force when you were coming out of a corner. A lot of times after being forced to let go, you'd go crashing into the sideboards.

The rink guards did not like that, and we got booted out of the rink a lot of times for doing it.

Though I never skated much again after my early teen years – I still have my father's skates from when he skated at competition level in the early 70s – I'll always remember how much I loved that weird feeling you would get after roller skating for hours; when you took your skates off, you felt like you were still gliding along as you walked.

I was starting to do more adult-like things, while still being a kid. I was becoming bolder in my actions, and testing the outside world in a more aggressive way than I ever had before. I was becoming physically bigger and I began to challenge the world in a way that sometimes frightened me; at the same time, I was pushing aside those feelings, seeking out more dangerous ways to fulfill my ever growing need for adventure.

I'm Not Getting in That Trunk

On that hot August Friday night, right around dusk, a bunch of us were out driving, looking for something to do. At the corner of Ellis Park Road and Bloor Street, there was an old fashioned gas station left over from the 50s. The station was still operational, and we stopped in for gas.

With me were Valerie, Denise and her 17-year-old boyfriend Charlie, and Charlie's friend Matt, who was also 17. The girls were already 14, so I'm the youngest. Both Charlie and Matt were from Etobicoke, me and the girls were from Swansea. Charlie's car was a blue 1968 four-door Chevy Biscayne. It was a little beat up, but it ran fine and was very fast. Four on the floor and a 427 big block turbo-jet rocket engine with 390 horsepower. When Charlie hit the pedal, it went where you wanted it to go, as long as it was a straight line; it wasn't so good on cornering. We gassed up and started driving south down Ellis Park Road. As we got to the path on the left that leads into High Park, Valerie, who was sitting in the back with me and Matt, asked Charlie to pull over.

Charlie questions her on this and Valerie says she has a fun idea. Charlie pulls the big car over to the side of the road, shuts off the motor, turns around to Valerie and says, "What? What's gonna be so funny?"

Valerie says, "One of the speakers is out of the back seat deck and there's a big hole there."

"So?" Charlie says.

"So... we roll all the windows down. Todd gets into the trunk, and then we drive around real slow. When we pass anyone walking on the street, we let Todd know, and he bangs on the trunk lid and starts screaming like he's being kidnapped."

"Brilliant," says Charlie. "Todd, get in the trunk, it'll be a hoot!"

"Fuck, no way. I'm not getting in that trunk. It's a fucking mess in there. I'll get grease all over my new white shirt, no!"

"I cleaned out the whole trunk last week; you could eat a five-course meal in there."

"I'm not getting in that trunk; I don't care how clean you say it is. What happens if the lock seizes? How do I get out then?"

"The trunk lock won't seize, but if it does, we can get you out by pulling out the back seat and you climb out. I'll give ya five bucks!" Charlie says.

"C'mon Todd, it'll be fun." Charlie hands me a five-dollar bill.

"Ya, c'mon Todd, get in the trunk," everyone says at the same time.

I think for a few seconds, then, "What the hell, okay, I'll do it. But you're not getting the five bucks back."

Everyone laughs and I crawl into the trunk. As Charlie is about to close the trunk lid with me looking up at him, I tell him, "Drive slow. I don't want to get all beat up in here."

"Don't worry, it'll be fun."

"It better be," I say, as Charlie slams the trunk lid shut.

Valerie is laughing her head off and asks if I can hear her clearly. "Yes, I can hear you," I say.

Charlie starts up the car and we continue driving south on Ellis Park Road. Within 20 seconds, Valerie yells back to me that there's an older couple coming up on our right. She signals me to start screaming and banging on the trunk lid. I do it as we pass the older couple who are out for an early evening walk. As we pass the couple, I can hear them yelling, "Hey, what's going on in there?" We all laugh as Charlie hits the gas and we leave fast. We continue with our little teenage prank for another 30 minutes or so around the neighbourhood and we hit about three other people with our little joke.

Later on, we come down Morningside from the east and Valerie sees another older couple out for a walk. Valerie gives me the signal and I go into my act. As we pass this couple, Denise, who's in the front seat says, "Shit, that was my mom and dad, and I'm pretty sure they saw me."

"Really?" I say.

Denise says, "It was them for sure, and they saw me."

"Well, that's the end of that. I want out of the trunk now anyway."

Charlie pulls over at the top of Morningside at Lavinia and I get out of the trunk. It was fun, but we don't want Denise to get into any trouble. We later find out that it was Denise's parents and she caught heck for it.

"Well, what's next?" I say. "The night is young."

Mooning the Humber Theatre Crowd

Charlie suggests we drive out to the cemetery at Park Lawn Road. It's quiet and spooky this time of night, and it'll be fun. We all say fine, so we drive up Windermere to Bloor and make a left on Bloor on the way to the cemetery that's just past the west end of the Humber River Bridge. As we're driving, we pass the Humber Theatre on the north side of Bloor just past Jane Street where we see a large crowd waiting in line to see a film. As we're passing by the crowd, Denise says, "Todd, hang a moon at the crowd!"

"Sure," I say. "But we already passed them; we'll have to drive around again." I move over to the passenger side of the car while Charlie pulls a U-turn to get ready to drive by a second time. As we are approaching the crowd, I pull my pants down and moon the line of moviegoers from the back seat window. But there is no reaction. I tell Charlie to make another pass, but this time honk the horn as we pass. I pull down my pants for a second time and moon the crowd while Charlie honks the horn right as we're passing by. This time the whole crowd is looking into the street, pointing, yelling, and laughing! Success!

They Took Our Clothes!

On to the cemetery! We continue driving towards the cemetery, then across the Humber River Bridge into what was then Etobicoke, on our way to Park Lawn cemetery to finish out the night with more teenage hijinks.

When we drive into the cemetery, it's as we expected – hot, dark and quiet. No one is there.

We're driving around deeper into the cemetery and it's getting darker. Charlie stops the car and Denise says, "Todd, let's me and you get out and ride around on the hood of the car."

"Sure," I say.

We both get out and are about to get on the hood of the car, and Denise says, "Let's take our clothes off, I'm hot."

"Ha," I say. "I'm not that hot!"

"I'll do it if you will!"

I think for a second, and say, "What the heck, you strip first!"

So she does, and she's now buck naked.

"Now you."

"Okay," I say, and now we're both buck naked.

At this point, Valerie, Charlie, and Matt are laughing at us both. We throw our clothes into the car, run to the front, and hop on the hood of the car, holding onto the little lip at the windshield where the wipers disappear.

We drive around a little bit laughing and looking at each other. Then, for some reason, Charlie stops the car, and yells at us to get off the hood. We don't know why he wants us off the hood, but we do what he says. The second we're off the car, Charlie reverses, turns the car around, and before me and Denise can get back in the car, he takes off and drives farther into the cemetery, leaving us nude in the road.

The cemetery was silent after the car went out of view. Only the sound of the hot wind whistling through the trees remained, and soon it started to rain. Denise looked over at me and yelled, "They took our clothes. They took our friggin' clothes!" But she didn't say friggin'. I said nothing, I was in shock. I stood there looking at her and her looking at me, both of us in our birthday suits. All we could do was break into uncontrollable laughter.

After a few minutes of looking around and wondering what we were going to do, we saw car lights coming towards us. We ran and hid behind a headstone, hoping it wasn't the cops, wishing it was Charlie.

Well, wouldn't ya know it, it was the cops. Either someone had called them from one of the houses that line the south end of the cemetery because of all the noise we were making before, or we were unlucky and they were on normal patrol.

As the big taxi-yellow cop car came closer, we huddled down behind the headstone together. When the car was almost on top of us, a huge bright spotlight came on and illuminated the whole area. The spot hit us, but the car kept going. The cops left as quickly as they appeared.

Dripping wet from the heat and the rain, we started talking about what we were going to do next. We had no solution but to hope the others would come back and get us. There was no way they were going to leave us alone with no clothes. So we sat down on the wet grass to wait.

Just then, we saw car lights coming towards us, and we got back behind the headstone. The headlights were Charlie's car, creeping through the cemetery. We came out into the roadway. The car stopped, and Charlie got out and threw us our clothes. We quickly got dressed and piled into the car.

We both started screaming at Charlie, Matt, and Valerie. "Why the heck did you leave us with no clothes? In a fucking graveyard!" Charlie said how he only meant to be a minute or two for a joke when he left us. But when he went around a bend to come back, he saw the cops and took off. They waited hidden, and when the cops left, they came back for us, hoping the cops didn't get us.

We both weren't happy about it, but it was an eventful night for sure. We were all tired and a little stressed from what had happened, so Charlie drove us all home, back into Swansea.

The next night, we went out and did it all again, just not the same stuff. It was a fun time, but I never did see either Charlie or Matt again after that summer of 1976.

True or False
Part I

1. Sometime in the early 70s, to allow for the playing of lacrosse in the summer, the decision was made to cover the dirt of the Rennie Park rink with concrete. Originally, the rink was a dirt floor with iron pipes laid horizontally along the length of the rink, about five or six inches above the ground. They would fill the rink with water and use the pipes to keep the ice frozen so you could play hockey. One summer, before the concrete was installed, a few buds and I climbed over the fence and started to fool around in the pipes-only rink. Somehow, I got my foot caught in between some of the pipes and I couldn't get it out. The cops and the fire department had to come and cut the pipes to free me. I was stuck there for about an hour.

2. When I was 10 years old, I made $125 in two hours as a foot model for a Toronto Parks & Recreation print ad for the High Park pool.

3. When I was 11 years old, a Swansea friend and I rode his mini bike, a Honda Mini-Trail 50, up and down the main hall of Swansea School on a Saturday for about an hour.

4. When I was 12 years old, two-litre glass bottles of Coke had just come onto the market. A few friends and I went to the Deforest Road variety store and bought one of the new bottles. One of my friends dared me to drink the whole bottle on our way back to the Rec Centre's pre-teen dance. By the time we had walked to just in front of the fire station on Deforest, I had finished about three-quarters of the bottle when I started feeling ill, and began to throw up while still walking. I would throw up on one side of the street, moaning, and then cross over and throw up on the other side of the street. This went on for about four or five street crossings before I had thrown up all the Coke I had drunk.

5. When I was 13 years old, my mom thought I was smoking. One day, she searched my room and found two cigarettes and a Cosmopolitan under the bed. With her hands firmly on her hips, she told my dad what she had found when he got home from work that evening – she did this right in front of me. This prompted my father to say, while looking quite perplexed, "How does Todd know how to make a Cosmopolitan?" Ha!

See Appendix B for detailed answers.

1F2F3T4T5F

41091

I skipped almost all of my first year of high school in 1976/1977. That first year I got 0.9 of a credit and missed more than three-quarters of the days, possibly more. I never got caught. How did I get away with it? Well, lemme tell ya.

I knew when you skipped school, they would call your house. I certainly never thought of trying to stop the phone from ringing when I skipped school at the time; that thought never entered my mind. I just made sure there would be no one home on a day when I wanted to skip class. Phone answering machines were not common in those days; we did not have one, and we only had one phone.

One day a technician came to our house when our phone had a problem. While he was fixing it, I was watching him and saw him use a special number you could call, immediately hang up, then a few seconds later the phone would ring. After I saw him use that number, I thought to myself, *Well, that's interesting.*

I asked the technician how he did it, and he told me the special number was 41091. Right there I knew I had something.

A few days later when no one was home, I took the cover off the phone and tested the wiring inside using the special number to see if I could figure out how to get the phone to not ring. Even when I was young, I was a bit of a tech guy and I was enjoying the challenge. I disconnected each wire in turn, until I found the one that made the phone ring when there was an incoming call, but if disconnected, would still allow an outgoing call. I didn't want the caller to get a busy signal, I just wanted to have it continue ringing so they wouldn't keep calling back. I was amazed but proud of myself that I figured it out. The first time the phone didn't ring, a big smile came to my face.

The problem here was I wouldn't be able to remove the cover of the phone when anyone was around to disconnect the ring wire, then do it again to reconnect the wire. That was too cumbersome and not practical.

What I needed was a simple on/off switch – a single pole, single throw switch somewhere on the phone to easily and quickly turn the ringer on and off whenever I wanted without being seen. There was no way I could hide a switch on the phone. But, I had remembered reading in one of my brother's electronics magazines that some switches could be buttons. So, I drilled a small hole in the bottom of the phone and installed a little push button switch to the wire and mounted it almost flush with the bottom plate of the phone. Since the phone had little feet on it, no one would see the button, and it wouldn't be engaged by moving the phone around. You had to turn the phone over, or reach under, and push the button.

In the morning on a day I was going to skip school, at an opportune moment, I would quickly turn the phone over or reach under, and press the button. After I got home later that day, I would repeat that, and nobody ever knew. The little button was dull silver in colour, so it blended in and looked like it was part of the phone. With a quick push of the button, bingo, no ringing! Push it again, and the ringer would work again. No one ever saw the button or ever said anything to me about it. When I left high school I forgot about it and never used it again.

After I found out about the number, I told others about it. A few people I told already knew the number, so I wasn't the first person to know about it. But I may have been the first to use it to test the wiring to stop the ringing. I never told anyone about my little trick with the button, though. I was a sneaky one for sure.

Vic Edwards
And his Mom's '59 Vette

In the fall of 1977, I was in my second year of Grade 9 at Western Tech High School, having gotten only 0.9 of a credit the previous year due to skipping so many classes.

One day while hanging out at school, not attending classes, one of my friends, Vic Edwards, who was a cool, funny guy in Grade 11, rolls up in an old, beat-up, faded gold 1959 Corvette. He yells at me from the street, "Bueler, come down for a ride!"

I skip down the stairs of the school to Evelyn Crescent where Vic sits in the Vette, revving the engine. It's a hot day and the car has no top on it. I hop in, close the heavy door with a clunk, and ask Vic where he got the car. He tells me it's his mom's.

"Ya, right," I say. But I did find out later from a mutual friend that it was his mother's car. He revs the engine again, pops the clutch, and the tires start smoking as we scream north up the street with all the nearby students yelling, whooping, and hollering.

We drive around the school a few times, sometimes racing up the streets, sometimes driving slowly, turning heads all the while. On our third pass up Evelyn Crescent, the vice principal of the school appears out of nowhere and walks right into the middle of the road in front of us. Vic gears down, puts the pedal to the floor, and the rear end gets a little away from him and slides out to the right as he cranks the wheel and swerves, missing the vice principal by inches. At this point, I'm just holding onto the dashboard grab bar in front of me for dear life.

We continue roaring up the street, make a quick right, then another quick right before stopping on the other side of the school on Evelyn Avenue. Vic tells me I better get out, so I hop out of the little sports car and run up the stairs to the rear of the school as Vic squeals away.

I run over to some friends I see sitting on a bench and sit down beside them. A few seconds later, I see the vice principal marching towards us from the west side of the school. He stops at the bench, points at me, and says, "Bueler! Were you just in that car racing around the school?"

"Who, me sir? No sir, I've been sitting here all morning."

My friends are all silent, staring at me with looks of, *Oh boy, you're gonna catch heck now, Bueler*.

"Well, it looked like you. If I ever catch you racing around the school in a car, you're in big trouble. I'm sure you have class to attend?"

"Yes, sir."

"Well then, get to it, boy!"

"Yes, sir."

The next day, I was booted out of school for drinking beer in the back of the cafeteria. I never returned and I never saw Vic again. I had just turned 15.

Booted Out of School For Good at 15

Not many of the people I have met, know, or worked with in my long career know this about me – I left school early in life, at age 15. I had skipped almost the whole first year of high school. The second year, I skipped the first two weeks and was booted out of Western Tech High School in the third week for drinking beer in the back of the school, and for not attending classes. It's not something I'm proud of, but it happened.

Why was I skipping school at such a young age? Was I having problems at home? No, my relationships with my parents and my three brothers were fine at the time. It's much simpler than that. I hated school and I was able to skip classes with little to no consequences. But that came to a quick end in my second year of high school.

Western Tech was about a mile from my house and Humberside Collegiate was about another half mile farther. Both schools are smack dab in the middle of a densely populated, residential area, an idyllic setting for high schools. A few of my friends and my future wife went to Humberside. I would meet up with my friends on the way to school and we would have a great time together – on the days I went to school, that is.

The student cafeteria is located in the back of the school. It's a big cafeteria that can serve over 1000 students at once. Right outside of the cafeteria, there are two tennis courts and some benches to the side partially covered over with trees and bushes. This was where I would hang out with my friends a lot of the time; we called it "The Back of the Caf." Teachers would walk through the area on occasion, but if the school's vice principal walked through, he was looking for someone. If he saw you and you weren't supposed to be there at that time, you were in trouble. The whole area was up one level from the street on the east side of the school, and it was a busy place, with lots of students coming and going, hanging around and milling about, so it wasn't isolated or desolate in any way.

Why?

Why did I leave school so early in life? I've thought a lot about that over the years, and well, it all comes down to the fact that I didn't care about school. I knew I would rather hang out with my friends or stay at home and sleep or read all day. I was never rebellious nor was I consciously trying to be. Rebelling was not something I thought about. I was not a rebel; I think the word renegade fits better. I did what I wanted and didn't care too much about the consequences.

I was not trying to make any kind of statement. I didn't pay attention to adults or what they were doing. At this time in my life, I had little interaction with adults other than teachers or my parents. I did not deliberately do things just to make them angry or shock them, but my actions did make that happen from time to time. That was a natural consequence of living in a way that may not always be the most popular. It's very natural to go along with the crowd for most. For me, it's natural to not go along with the crowd. My actions were rarely straight-out defiance. I lived life on my own terms, and some may define that as rebellion, but it wasn't that at all.

During those years, I hated it when anyone interfered or tried to interfere with what I did. In my mind, what I did was my business. It's not that I wasn't aware of how much what I sometimes did affected others. I was fully aware, but I always tried to not act willy-nilly when I knew my actions may cause discomfort to others. I knew I wasn't living in a bubble. So although I did pretty much what I wanted, I understood the potential impact of my actions on others, and tried to mitigate that impact as much as possible. I didn't act with self-impunity. I think the story below expresses this best.

I was streamed into a Level 4 technical high school, when I should have been put into a Level 5 academic high school. I hated, and was terrible at all the shop classes, from wood shop to auto shop, welding to sheet metal, etc.

I loved and was good at English, history, math, and social studies, I also liked electricity. I did like the techie stuff and that could have been the math guy in me. I preferred reading and writing over working with my hands, which I was never good at anyway. If I had to build a house, it would turn out like the fun house at the carnival, with wavy floors and crooked windows.

Clean out Your Locker

After my first year of high school, where I missed almost three quarters of my classes, I had to repeat Grade 9. I returned to school in the fall of 1977, and had turned 15 during the first week of school that year. I skipped the full first two weeks, and in the middle of the third week, I was still not attending any classes. I was hanging out at The Back of the Caf with my friends, who were also skipping classes. It was about 1 p.m. and we were sitting on a bench near the tennis courts with a case of beer under one of the benches. We were drinking the beer discreetly, joking, laughing, and having a great time. Then, out of nowhere, the vice principal appeared at the top of the stairs that led down to the street on the east side of the school.

There was no time to react; he was on us in a few seconds. He saw the beer case under the bench and saw I had an open beer in my hand. He was gunning for me this time, for sure, as he walked straight up to me and said, "Bueler, drinking beer on school grounds again, eh?" I said nothing.

Then he said, "Bueler, put that beer back in the case. You're coming to the office with me. The rest of you get back to class or you're going to have more trouble than you already do."

I put the open beer back into the case as my friends all got up and scooted away. Then he reached down under the bench and picked up the case of beer. "Let's go, Todd," he said. The renegade in me, just for a second, thought maybe I'd tell him to "F-off" and then walk off school grounds.

But for some reason I didn't, and I went with him to the school office.

The school was very big with a lot of students and the halls were quite wide. As we entered the school, the bell had just rung for class change and the halls were flooded with students and teachers. There were lots of thumbs up, shouts of, "Way to go, Bueler!" from the other students, and head shaking from teachers as we made our way through the labyrinth of halls to the school office area. The vice principal did not say a single word to me or to any of the other students as we pushed our way through them.

When we got to his office, he put the beer case down outside the door and told me to go inside and sit down. As I sat down in front of his desk, he turned to leave and told me to stay put, closing the door behind him. *Oh boy, I'm in for it now,* I thought to myself. I didn't know what he had planned for me, but I had a pretty good idea. I was thinking, *this was it for me at this school. The End. I was going to be expelled.*

The vice principal returned about 10 or 15 minutes later with some papers in his hand. He sat down at his desk and told me I was finished at this school.

"What does that mean?" I asked.

He said, "You're done here. You're out of the school. I'm expelling you."

"Why?"

"Well, let's have a look at your record, shall we? You did not attend classes for most of the last school year." Then he looked at some of his papers and continued, "In fact, last year you were absent a total of 137 days or 75% of the time. This year, you have attended school a total of... zero, zero days. You didn't show up for a single class this year! Do you have anything to say for yourself?"

"Nope," I said.

"And then there's the beer drinking on school property. Todd, you're 15 years old. It's illegal to drink alcohol at your age. You know this, right?"

"Yes, I know that."

"And... It's also against school rules to drink alcohol on school property. I presume you also know this?"

"Yes, I do."

"This isn't the first time you have been caught drinking beer on school property."

"No, I guess it isn't."

"Well then, do we need to go on?"

"No."

"The school has not been able to get in touch with your parents, either by phone, or by mail."

Well, that would be because I cut the phone off to incoming calls during the day, and I also intercepted any mail coming from the school, so my parents didn't see the letters, I said to myself.

"You're going to clean out your locker right now and leave the school property. Do not come back to this school. Do you understand? When you get home, you're going to give this letter to your parents and see if you can get into another school. That's it. Goodbye, Todd. I wish you luck in the future."

During this whole exchange, not once did he show me any empathy or concern. He was cold and a bit harsh throughout, but I couldn't have cared less. As far as I was concerned, I was done with school. I hated everything about it, except seeing my friends, and the few classes I liked – English and history, to be specific. I took the letter and as I was walking out of his office, he stopped me and said, "If I don't hear back from your parents within one week, I will have no choice but to send truancy officers to your house. Please, make sure your parents get the letter." I took the letter and left his office to go clean out my locker.

Of course, I opened and read the letter the second I walked out of his office. It said something to the effect of, "Your son has been expelled. Please contact me as soon as possible." I never returned to Western Tech after that day.

Walking in the Rain and Animals

As I walked home, it started to rain, not hard, just a drizzle. When I got home, I was tired, wet, and cold, and no one was home. I pushed the button on the bottom of the phone to allow incoming calls to come back in (see the "41091" story in this book for an explanation of this "button"). I went upstairs into my brother's room, lit up a smoke, and put Pink Floyd's *Animals* album on his stereo – not loud, but at a nice listening level. I was a little stressed out and the warmth of the vinyl music was calming to me. About 10 minutes into side one of the album, and in the middle of the song "Dogs," I heard the phone ring downstairs. I ran down and stared at the phone for a few seconds before answering it, wondering who could be calling in the middle of the day? It was the vice principal.

"Hello?"

"Is this Todd? This is Mr. Osbourne. Are either of your parents at home?"

"Yes, this is Todd. No, my parents aren't home."

"Well, you need to give them the letter and tell them I'll call again tomorrow."

"I will."

I hung up the phone and thought nothing of the call. I went back upstairs, lit up another smoke, and finished listing to Pink Floyd. He didn't call back the next day.

I showed the letter to my parents that night. They were not too happy about it, but I will say they weren't as upset as I thought they would be. They tried to talk me out of staying out of school, but I had decided I wanted to work full time and would not go back. I didn't get much of an argument from my parents and I got a job the very next week. I had to go to family court with my mom to get approval to stay out of school since I wasn't the legal age of 16 to quit. There was almost no argument from the judge either. The adults involved were so matter-of-fact throughout the whole ordeal, and by ordeal, I mean from the expulsion to the approval to quit school permanently at age 15. The responses from the adults were, "You don't want to return to school? No problem, that's fine with us." No fighting, no yelling, no, "Now Todd, you do know if you leave school now, life may become difficult for you in the future?" There was none of that – no advice, no guidance, and no direction. I will say my parents were the only ones who showed me any empathy or care.

What did I think of it all? I thought it was great and the best thing that could have happened to me. Of course, I was completely wrong. I thought, *I'm gonna buy a new Levi's jean jacket. I'm gonna buy a car. I'm gonna buy a dirt bike. I'm gonna buy a guitar!* Well, I got the jean jacket and the car, a two-door '62 T-Bird with a big 390 V8 engine that I bought with a loan from my grandmother within a week of leaving school. I bought the dirt bike the year after, and I bought a Gibson Les Paul guitar the year after that. I paid more for the guitar than I did for the car. The jean jacket, the car, and the dirt bike are all long gone, but I still have the guitar. Was I let down by the system and all the adults around me? Sure, but that's where I found myself at the time – it was the fall of 1977. Leaving high school before graduating was not out of the ordinary for those times growing up in Swansea.

Most of the people I grew up with never made it past Grade 10. Nancy and I are the only ones we know of amongst our friends, who later in life went on to complete college, after leaving high school without graduating.

I went to work in a medium-sized printing shop downtown (see "The Working Life of a 70s Teenager" story in this book for more about my time there). About two years in, I was starting to get bored with running a printing press and started to look for different kinds of work. I liked working at the print shop, the people there were all very nice, and I had a lot of fun over those two and a half years. But in the end, the work wasn't intellectually stimulating enough for me, and I slowly began to hate going to work. I needed more mentally challenging work and running a machine was not cutting it.

For years, I jumped in and out of jobs – in a factory, driving, and at other print shops after leaving that first one. Somewhere in my heart, I knew this low-level employment was not for me. I found that at every job I had, I learned much more quickly than the people around me, and I got bored. I would up and quit these jobs. In fact, I used to walk out the door in the middle of the day with no notice. Initially, I wouldn't even care about the money owed to me, but I did eventually call and go get my last paycheques.

I tried to go back to night school many times, but for some reason, it never worked out. I continued to work at jobs I hated while trying out different things along the way.

The printing jobs weren't factory jobs with assembly lines or stand-alone work stations, where materials were delivered to your work station and you had to assemble the parts into a product. They were semi-factory jobs, but skilled, and the buildings were called plants, not factories. In the printing plants where I worked, you wouldn't work with only one press; sometimes you would have to run bigger, more complicated printing presses too. I also worked at mailing houses running mass mailing machines, industrial paper folding machines, and collating machines. These were also semi-factory, but more accurately, the jobs were skilled with a sort of factory feel to them.

Between working at printing plants and mailing houses, the jobs/careers I tried included being a stockbroker, which entailed having to take and pass the incredibly difficult Canadian Securities Course. I also worked as a private chauffeur for a wealthy man who lived downtown. I tried working as a courier/truck driver at UPS, though this was not for me, and I lasted one day. After doing 110 stops with mostly big, heavy packages, I came home with bruises all over my biceps; I even worked as a pizza delivery guy for about six months for Yum Yum Pizza on Bloor Street.

None of these options worked out and I found myself always going back to running a printing press. It was what I knew, it was highly paid, and I was good at it, but I hated it. I could always get a printing job whenever I needed or wanted one. There was no shortage of that type of job in the marketplace at the time. This went on until I was 24, when I decided to make a concerted effort to go back to school and get an education no matter what obstacles I was facing. I couldn't go on with the way things were any longer. That story, called "Return to School," can be found later in this book.

The Working Life of a 70s Teenager

In the fall of 1977, at age 15, I went to work for $2.75 an hour, which was ten cents an hour over minimum wage at the time. The job was in a printing and mass mailing shop in downtown Toronto at Church and Richmond Streets. In the Toronto of the 1970s, everything was old and musty, with few exceptions. One such exception was the Bloor-Danforth subway line I rode to get to work. It was opened by the Toronto Transit Commission (TTC) in 1966 and runs east and west along Bloor Street and Danforth Avenue. I would travel east on this "Bloor line" from Runnymede station in Swansea and get off at the Yonge station where I would transfer to the Yonge-University subway line and go south to Queen station. The TTC opened this north-south subway line in 1954, and I rode in the original red subway cars which were affectionately called the "Red Rockets."

Taking the subway to work reminded me of a time just a few years earlier. On Sundays in the early 70s, when I was 10 or 11, my friends and I had to make our own fun. So, we would pay the 10 cent fare to get on the subway, and ride the Yonge-University line. We liked the old red trains, and those trains only ran on that line.

As we rode to every stop, the inside lights of the trains would flicker on and off, the heavy trains would shake from side to side, and the steel wheels would shriek and screech when it went around a sharp corner. If you were sitting too close to your friends, your heads would clunk together.

We'd get off the train at each stop, run up the stairs from the platform, push the big button on the transfer machine, and with a loud mechanical *da-dunk* sound, the machine would spit out a paper transfer. We repeated this until we had collected a transfer from every station. It was a much simpler time in my life.

The subway was a means of entertainment for me then, but it became a matter of practicality. I tried to avoid it as much as possible; it was more of an expense choice rather than about convenience. If I could afford to drive to work every day, I would. The switch from being a child to being a teenager happened so fast, and a lot had changed.

The city was clean, but old for the most part. Everything was so... mechanical. Many of the buildings were made of wood, brick, and cinder block. However, not everything was old. In addition to the Bloor-Danforth subway, there was the new bank towers downtown.

The print shop where I worked was in an old three-storey industrial warehouse-style building. It smelled like the old cottages in northern Ontario when they were first opened for the summer season after being closed all winter. It had wavy wooden floors and a freight elevator that carried finished mailing and print jobs, the tons of paper we used, and barrels of harsh cleaning solvents we used to clean the presses. These harsh chemicals can and do wreak havoc on your hands. Years later, when I was trying to leave the printing business, but still had to take printing jobs to pay the bills, it got to the point where my hands were so badly damaged, I had to sleep wearing rubber surgical gloves after coating my hands with high-end, super moisturizing hand cream with 5% cortisone – it was very painful. The damage to my hands eventually healed in my mid-20s after I stopped running printing presses for good.

That freight elevator could carry a lot, but it had its limits. I remember on more than one occasion when we were afraid the elevator wouldn't carry the amount of weight we put in it. Sometimes it would sink a few inches below floor level when we would put in just one more skid. A red warning light and a short siren would go off if the elevator was overweight, and it wouldn't operate, so we would have to unload it until the warning stopped. It wasn't the most secure elevator. Some of my co-workers would disconnect the overweight warning lights and siren so they could stuff it full, but I never got on it when they did that.

I worked there for just over two and a half years. I started out as a messenger boy, moved up to a shipping clerk, then on to running the mailing machines, and finally learning how to run the printing presses. While I worked as a messenger boy, the only new construction I saw in downtown Toronto was the First Canadian Place skyscraper at Bay and King Streets, which was completed in the summer of 1975. I would often go up to its 73rd floor to pick up artwork for a printing job or deliver a small sample of a job for approval.

By the time I was running the presses, I was highly skilled and making $5.00 an hour. Amongst my group of friends who had also left school early, I was making almost twice the amount of money they were making at their factory jobs. As a result, I almost always had a car. Downtown parking was expensive, and the price of gas for the big V8 engines in the first few cars I had was high, so I didn't drive to work every day. About two or three days a week, I would walk the half mile from my house up to the subway so I could ride the train to work. The ridership volume on the subway back then was a lot lower than it is today, so I always got a seat, and the service was reliable. Even with that, I hated taking the subway to work and preferred to drive.

Each day I would get up and get dressed in the standard Canadian teenage attire of the 1970s: jeans, a jean jacket, t-shirt, and running shoes. In the winter, the wardrobe would be the same except for either tan construction boots or winter boots. If it was really cold, I would throw on a flannel shirt, but never a sweater, and the jean jacket was replaced with a navy-blue, nylon-shelled, four pocket snorkel parka with an orange lining.

After I was promoted into the printing department, I almost never saw my boss, the head of printing. This guy was a real 1960s/1970s old school guy. I'm talking coffee, cigarettes, cigars, and a half bottle of hooch with two glasses in the top drawer of his desk; I never once saw him eat. He would offer you a snort when you went into his office for a meeting, and I always took him up on that. I would see him smoking and drinking coffee each morning, as his office looked out onto Richmond Street through a big picture window right where I came in to punch my timecard.

My boss was a great guy; he was always calm, and he pretty much left us alone to do our work. The only interaction I had with him was at raise time, or when he saw me as he was walking around the plant sometimes, and he would ask me how everything was going. He did care about his employees though. In fact, the whole place was like that, except for the older women who worked in the bindery department, they pretty much kept to themselves. Almost everyone who worked at the plant was young – mostly teenagers and guys in their 20s. The bosses were older; they knew we were young and that our job wasn't the most important part of our lives. That didn't bother them, and they dealt with us in an empathetic way. Everyone was easygoing and there was always a lot of laughing and fooling around.

Normal work hours were Monday to Friday, 8:30 a.m. to 5 p.m. with an hour for lunch, and they would only dock our pay if we were 15 minutes late, but most of the time they didn't even enforce that rule.

Though the heads of other departments were not my direct superiors, I did sometimes take direction from them. At times, when I was a messenger boy, the bosses would play pranks on me. They would try to send me out to Aikenhead's Hardware store on Temperance Street to get a sky hook, or a paper stretcher, but I never fell for it. One time, though, I played along and said okay. I went to the store, and when I came back, I told my boss I had paid for the paper stretcher with the company credit card, but it was too heavy for me to carry, so Aikenhead's was going to deliver it that afternoon. My boss ended up calling them to confirm the information, so I got him on that one!

We worked hard and sometimes we worked many, many hours per week. There were lots of opportunities for overtime and we were paid time and a half for any time worked over the 37.5 hours that made up the regular work week. If we worked on the weekend, we didn't have to come in until 9:30 or 10:00 in the morning. We also worked a lot of nights and weekends, and I remember working 21 days straight including overtime at night more than once. During those busy times, I was wiped out, and in the mornings, I would come into work feeling like I had left only a few hours before. There were many days where that was the case, but I was young, and I could handle it all.

Half of the shop was a mailing house, so there were big canvas mail bags stacked three feet high in the big room beside the main mailing work area on the third floor. When we worked on the weekends, most of us would be hung-over from the previous night. We would get to work between 9:30 and 10 a.m., set up our machines, and maybe run them for a short time, maybe not. After that we would leave the job floor and go into the big storage room and sleep on the stacks of mail bags for a few hours. We would wake up at noon, and if it was a Saturday, we would go to the bar next door for lunch and some beer for an hour or so, and then return to work till five o'clock in the evening.

Following those crazy stretches of overtime, I wouldn't come in on the following Monday. The bosses knew what was happening and didn't say anything on Tuesday except to ask if I was feeling better, as the big job had been completed, and it was back to a slower working pace.

Every Friday was payday. We got our paycheques at midmorning and just about every young guy in the shop would go out to the bank around the corner at noon to cash it. The line at the bank was always crazy and we were in there for half an hour most times. Then most of the guys would go over to the Windsor Tavern, which was right beside the plant, for lunch and beer.

The Windsor Tavern was an old establishment built in the 1880s, and you knew that the second you walked in. The bar itself was on the second floor and the stairs were uneven and made of wood. It was dark inside, smelled like stale beer and cigarettes, had old tables with wobbly chairs, and the draft beer was 25 cents a glass. If it was a sunny day, you would be blind for a while when you first walked inside until your eyes adjusted.

As I was the new guy, and the youngest, it was my job to go back to the plant and punch in everyone's timecard at 1 p.m. Afterwards, I would return to the pub to drink beer with my co-workers. We would stay in the bar until about 3 p.m. or later, unless there was a job with a tight deadline. Sometimes the bosses were there with us, and knew about us punching back in, but we never got docked for it. A meeting was called one Monday, and we were all told the practice had to stop. Of course, it continued, and it was never brought up again.

That workplace was a dying breed, even in those days. It was the best job I ever had, and I never did work at a job like that again. I'm pretty sure no workplace like this exists anywhere anymore.

Eventually my boss in the printing department left the company over some disagreement with the owners, one of whom was his brother in Montreal. My old boss in the mailing department ended up taking over the printing department. This guy was a little tougher, but he still pretty much left you alone.

Then Along Came Sophie…

My French girlfriend's name was Sophie. She was fully bilingual; when she spoke, it was the sexiest sound you ever heard. Her accent was French-Canadian but refined. She sounded exotic like she was from Paris and not Montreal; she was "Paree" through and through. She had the biggest brown eyes with long, thick, wavy, chestnut brown hair. When she looked at you with those big brown eyes, you could not deny her anything she asked of you – and I never did. She was neither thin nor heavy, she was just knockout gorgeous. She was 15 and I was 16. I had been working at the plant for a year at this point.

She was in love with me, and I fell in love with her. She was also the boss' daughter. Sophie wasn't my first love, but at the time I felt like she was.

My first love was a Swansea girl named Angie, when I was in Grade 6 in 1973, and she was in Grade 5. Angie dumped me in the cloakroom at the top of the stairs on the second floor of the Swansea Recreation Centre. A lot of kissing went on in that cloakroom. She told me I wasn't ever serious, and everything was always a joke to me. She was very mature for a girl of only 10, and of course I was an 11-year-old super immature boy. I asked her not to dump me and told her I would change for her, but she didn't go for it. I remember her being empathetic towards me, shaking her head knowing I didn't understand, and that was the end of my first love.

Over the next few weeks, I tried and tried to get her back, but it was no use; I had lost her forever. I lost my first love being happy-go-lucky Todd, and I didn't know what being serious meant at that age. Was it puppy love, or real love? At age 11, I tend to think it was the former. Looking back now at all that happened then, all I can say is, I was a fool. I saw Angie again decades later. We had coffee and talked about old times, but of course she wasn't the 10-year-old girl who I was in love with back then. I still think about her sometimes, all these years later.

My second love was another Swansea girl named Valerie; this was during the second half of Grade 6 in the late winter or early spring of 1974. We had a great relationship and laughed a lot together, but Valerie broke up with me a few months later, right before the end of school that year. Despite the breakup and all the years since, we are still friends to this day. We have spoken about it during the writing of this book, and neither of us can remember the reason she broke up with me, but we do both remember the breakup happening at the top of the Willard Park stairs that day. Valerie had broken my heart for the first time in my life. I cried for days on end. It took me a long time to recover. Does anyone ever recover from true love that is broken?

I didn't fall in love again until I was 16, with Sophie. In the end, I lost Sophie too. I've always gotten what I wanted in life, but I haven't always been able to keep it.

Sophie worked in the bindery department on the first floor with her mother, while I ran the presses on the second floor. She would make excuses to come up to the second-floor press room to see me for a few minutes, and I did the same to go downstairs to see her, if only for a short time.

It was early in the spring of 1979 when she came to work at the plant – a couple of days a week at first, as she was still in school. By late spring, we were boyfriend and girlfriend. We spent as much time together as we could, all the while hiding our relationship from her father. We would get lunch together and walk through the downtown parks hand in hand every day, stealing kisses from one another whenever we could, always on the lookout for her father who might be out on the streets, close to the plant. She would take me to French bookstores and read romantic novels to me in French, and then she would translate for me.

Fridays were slow days at the plant, and most people had long lunches, leaving the plant almost empty for hours. After Sophie came, I stopped going to the bar on Fridays, and we would sneak away to the second-floor storage area where no one ever went. The storage area took up almost half the width of the building. It was quiet and warm with stacks and stacks of big, industrial-sized canvas mail bags, piled about four feet high in the back of the big storage room. There was no noise except for the traffic from the street two storeys below. We would talk and neck and some other things a gentleman doesn't talk about, but we never went further. Not that I didn't want to, but we were both young and in love, and it wasn't right doing that in the storage room of a printing plant on a stack of old canvas mail bags. Neither of us pushed on it; there would be lots of time for that.

As I mentioned previously, Sophie worked with her mother on the first floor. Her mother only spoke French, so while I did see her mother from time to time, I never spoke with her. One day while I was on the first floor getting something, her mother looked right at me and smiled a lovely smile. She had never given me a second look before that day. I thought it was odd, but I gave her a smile right back; then she put her head down and got back to work.

I wondered if Sophie's mother knew about us, or if she was merely being polite? It bothered me and I wondered if I should ask Sophie if it meant anything.

The next day I got up enough courage to ask Sophie if her mother knew about us.

"Of course she knows," Sophie told me.

"Well, how did she find out?" I asked.

"I told her."

"You told her? Why would you do that? I could lose you and my job if your father finds out. You do know that, right?"

"It's not a big deal. My mother and I are close. I tell my mom everything, she tells my dad nothing. Don't worry about it, it's fine."

I didn't know how to take this or what to say, and I told Sophie my thoughts. Again, she told me not to worry and how we only needed to be careful. She told me her mother was happy she had a boyfriend, and she thought I was a very cute, sweet boy. Sophie told her mother I was both of those things and more, and she thought she was in love with me. That explained the smiles I got from her mother every time I saw her, it made me feel good. I was happy Sophie's mother liked me because I was making her daughter happy.

The end of summer was near, and I knew Sophie was going back to school. One day while we were lying on a stack of mail bags, she told me she was going back to Montreal after the summer.

"What? Why?" I asked, caught quite off guard.

She told me her parents were separating, and she and her mother were going back to Montreal. I was devastated.

"Is there anything I can do?" I asked her.

"Not unless you move to Montreal," she said. I was crushed.

In the fall of 1979, I turned 17. I was promoted at work downstairs to the first-floor main printing area where the bigger presses were. I got a big raise and started to run a more sophisticated two-colour printing press. This new position, along with another new interest of mine that was developing, took my mind off Sophie somewhat. That new interest was my future wife, Nancy.

Nancy

I need to back up a bit. In the spring of 1979, I wanted Nancy to be my girlfriend. The problem was, I had missed my chance by not being aggressive enough in pursuing her and she was already going out with another guy. He was a Swansea boy, but I didn't care; I wasn't going to wait any longer.

In mid-May, I called her on the phone as we were already friends and asked her to meet me at the corner bench in Rennie Park. When we met at the bench alone, she had no idea why I wanted to meet with her. It was a beautiful day, sunny, neither too hot, nor too cold, with the big yellow willow tree right in front of us swaying side to side in the warm, low wind. I asked her how it was going with her boyfriend, and she said it was going well. I asked her if she was happy with him, and she said she was.

I told her I didn't like the guy and that she should dump him for me. I told her I liked her a lot and I would treat her better than him. To my surprise, she wasn't mad at me, but she turned me down. I was cordial and told her to call me when they break up, I knew they would. I told her I would be waiting for her when that happened. "Just call me and I'll be right there for you," I said. She didn't say anything after that, but her attitude changed. She looked at me warmly; I think she was in a bit of shock.

I knew the guy she was dating from around the neighbourhood. Though I had never hung out with him, I had seen him around. I knew that Nancy wasn't the same type of person as he was, and I knew it was only a matter of time before it ended with him. This time, I would make sure that I was there when opportunity struck.

During the summer of that year, I was thinking of Nancy all the time, but I was in a relationship with Sophie. Was I in love with Sophie or Nancy? I didn't know. I had Sophie, but I didn't have Nancy. I thought I was in love with Sophie, but I had doubts. This point bugged me all through that summer. One thing I do remember is how I couldn't stop thinking about Nancy, and every time I saw her, my heart would flutter. What would I do if Nancy broke up with her boyfriend? Would I go after her and forget about Sophie? It weighed on me. I was confused, very confused.

During my mid-teens in the 70s, the summers were always very hot. There were almost no private pools in Swansea; however there was one private pool that was easily accessible. Without the owner knowing, some friends and I would go to it late on hot summer nights and swim for an hour or so to cool off. I'm not going to say where it was for privacy reasons, as I believe the pool is still there.

We had already been to the pool two or three times that summer without a hitch. But this night would prove to be different.

It was the first Sunday in August after a very warm July. I was still 16, and about six weeks shy of becoming Nancy's boyfriend; but I had a bead on her since the spring. She was the one!

It had been an incredibly hot day, mid-90s°F with the humidity, and the temperature hadn't come down much by the time nightfall came. It was still in the high 70s or low 80s when we reached the back yard fence just before 10 p.m.

Nancy and I were both there, along with four other Swansea friends; one of Nancy's girlfriends and three other guys. The previous times we were at the pool, the gate had been unlocked. This night it seemed to be locked, as two of the boys couldn't get the gate open and hopped over the fence. As I was climbing over, my cut-off jeans got caught on the top of the fence, and I landed hard head-first onto the dirt ground. I had a huge bump on the side of my head and a sore neck.

I got up and was about to help the girls over the fence, when Nancy tried the gate one last time before she started to climb over. Well, wouldn't you know it, the gate wasn't locked at all, just a little stuck. Both girls called us boys dumb as we were all laughing about the whole thing, then she opened the gate, and walked right in.

Nancy asked me if I was okay. I smiled at her romantically, and as I was rubbing my head and in a soft voice, I said, "I'm fine." She tilted her head a little, looking at me strangely for a second or two, and then hugged me and said, "Good."

After swimming for an hour or so, trying to be as quiet as teenagers could be, the owner of the house, a middle-aged woman, appeared at one end of the pool wearing an old housecoat. It was dark, and we didn't see her.

She walked right up to the pool and said in a nice, calm voice, "I don't mind you kids swimming in my pool at night. But you have to keep it clean. You can come and swim here anytime you like if you sometimes come and clean the pool for me."

We were all in a bit of shock. We looked up to her and I said, "Of course, we'll be here tomorrow to help clean your pool."

She then said, "That would be fine," then turned around and walked back into her house. We showed up the next day and spent about an hour cleaning her pool.

We went back a few more times late at night after that to swim when it was hot, but we never saw that lady again. She never came out to the pool again, and we never went to her house to talk to her. But we did go back a few times to clean her pool for her.

Summer ended and Sophie left me, with lots of hugging and crying. The days after she left were difficult for me, and I stayed at home a lot doing nothing and sleeping all the time. I never did see or hear from Sophie again.

During the third week of September, I found out Nancy had broken up with her boyfriend. I had bided my time and was always a gentleman. Nancy was the one. Nothing would stop me from winning her over. I wanted Nancy – no two ways about it. I knew I would get her, as I always got what I wanted, though I couldn't always keep what I had. I couldn't be stopped when I wanted something, but I couldn't take another loss in love. This time, no matter what, I was going to get that girl and I was going to keep her. I lost Angie, I lost Valerie, and I lost Sophie. I had had enough; it wouldn't happen again. The second I heard about the breakup, I swooped in and saved her from her broken heart, like a white knight. I walked over to her house and knocked on the door. Nancy answered the door, and she knew why I was there. I didn't even have to ask her. She looked at me and said, "Yes, I'll go out with you." I quickly kissed her on the cheek before she had a chance to move away. She put her hand to her cheek and giggled. I told her I'd call her later and I left, skipping all the way home. I didn't have to worry about missing Sophie anymore; Nancy had fixed that problem for me.

Both Nancy and I have long and deep family roots in Swansea. We have both lived here our whole lives. The only exception was when we first moved out together at age 21 to live for a short time in a small apartment in south Etobicoke. Nancy was born in Toronto and had lived in the same house in Swansea her whole life until we moved, for that short time. Eventually we moved back to Swansea and still live here today.

Nancy's family has a much longer Swansea history than mine. Her family roots in Swansea go back more than 130 years. Nancy lived on Morningside Avenue, and I lived on Lavinia Avenue. I knew her from early childhood at school, and from the neighbourhood. We both attended Swansea School from kindergarten till Grade 8. We were in the same class for Grades 5, 6, and 8. I'm not sure when we first met, but there were no childhood play dates. We didn't interact socially until we were older. I played a little shinny hockey with her older brother, so I had been to her house as a kid, but we weren't in the same crowd.

At about age 14, right after we entered high school, we found ourselves in the same crowd. Nancy's house was a bit of a hangout spot for our small group of friends. It was near Rennie Park, and it was a good size too, so I spent some time there with our friends.

We were only friends at first, but over the next few years I started to notice her in a different way. She was the prettiest girl in the neighbourhood and I was always looking at her when we would all hang out together. She was funny and so full of life. She was observant about what was happening around her and I think she knew I liked her. While she could be naive at times, she was a loyal, trusting girl. She was open about things and never played any stupid social head games. She was up-front, honest, and laughed a lot. We went out on our first date a few days after I knocked on her door after her breakup, and eight years later we were husband and wife; we've been together ever since.

My dad on the right, circa 1946, age 18. My uncle Norm, his brother, on the left. Car is a 1938 Ford Deluxe V8. I don't know where the photo was taken.

My mom on the left, in her competition roller skating outfit, circa 1948. The brick house on the left is my childhood home, 85 Lavinia Ave. Dig that 40s hairstyle. She would be married within a year at age 18.

Another shot of my Mom, same day as the previous photo.

My dad running and programming a UNIVAC 9200 Computer. Circa 1964, Age 36 in Toronto. Punchcard stacker on the bottom right. He had four kids by then. It must have been a stressful time in his life.

IBM Data Centre, King Street, Toronto 1968. My dad worked here as a programming supervisor from the early 1960s until the mid-1970s. Photo Courtesy of IBM Archives. Photographer George Dunbar.

My father's Science award, 1946. Age 18, Grade 12, De La Salle High School Avenue Road, Toronto. I believe you needed an over 90% average in all science classes for your final year. My dad was one smart cookie.

My mom holding me, age about 7 months. Spring, 1963 at the Aurora house.

My first year in Swansea Hockey House League, 1969/1970.

Team MVP Swansea Hockey House League, 1973/1974.
Poke Check Kid Story.

School picture day, 1969. I'm the second kid from the right, top row.

Swansea Hockey House League. Circa 1971/1972 season. This was on the Deforest Road side of the Swansea Legion Branch #46 on Durie St during the banquet in the spring. I'm the tallest guy on the right. I would have been 9 years old. The team's sponsor was Cecil Ward's Men Shop. Our jerseys were bright orangey/red with yellow writing.

Swansea Hockey House League. Circa 1974 at Rennie Park Rink. I'm second from the right, bottom row, age 12.

Me at age 10, in front of my house on Lavinia Ave. With my good friend Jeanette, and furry friend. Summer 1973.

Pool, Billiards, 8 Ball, 9 Ball
And a Hundred Bucks

I was a teenage pool shark. A pool hustler, at 15. But I only did it once. Well... twice. And I won, big time! Well, big time for a 15 year old in the 70s. Other than the following story, I never played pool for money.

The guys I took deserved it. They were hustlers, but me and my buddy were better. It all started in the pool room of the condo building at 35 Ormskirk in South Swansea, in the late fall of 1977. It ended in a pool hall at Bloor Street and Royal York Road a few weeks later.

My pool hall partner was a friend of mine, Mitch, who lived in the condo at the time.

It was a cold fall day. It wasn't blustery, only a little windy, with the leaves already beginning to change colour and fall from the trees. My buddy had called around noon and asked what I was doing.

"Just sittin' around," I said.

He asked if I wanted to come down to his place and play some ping pong, maybe some pool. He said he had some beers.

"Of course," I said. "I'll be down in an hour." It was a Sunday.

The Life of a 1970s Teenager

A Little Background

Playing Pool at the Swansea Rec Centre

The Swansea Rec Centre on Lavinia Ave, a few doors from my house, was the place where we spent a lot of time in the 70s as kids. It was open year-round. There were no video games or other technological home entertainment then like there is today, and we had almost no homework, so when we weren't in school, we had a lot of free time. We had few household chores to do other than shovel the snow or cut the grass on occasion, and besides a paper route, kids didn't have part time jobs then either.

During the winter and cooler months, other than going to a friend's house or skating at the Rennie Park rink, it was about the only place we went to spend our time. One of the most popular places at the Rec Centre was the games room on the top floor, and it took up the full south end of the building. It had ping pong tables, shuffleboard, a foosball table, a couple of card tables, and a pool table. There were large windows on the south, east, and west walls. The most popular game for me and my friends was pool. Not everyone liked pool, so it wasn't hard to be on the table for most of the day or evening.

We played for hundreds of hours – weekday evenings, most of the day on some Saturdays, and on Sunday afternoons. When you play one game for that amount of time, year in and year out, you tend to get very, very good at it, and some of my friends and I did just that. Pool was not the only thing we did as teenagers, but it was the main form of entertainment for more than a few of us.

I remember how a couple of friends and I were always there on weekends. We waited at the front door for the Rec Centre to open at 9:30, then we ran up the stairs and walked into the games room. If we were there at opening on Saturday mornings, it was cold, dark, and quiet as the supervisor went about opening the rest of the Rec Centre.

After about an hour, the big room would warm up from having been cold and empty all night. The lights would come on, and 70s Top 40 music would start to play through the sound system. These were the times I liked the best. No other kids were around, screaming, laughing, and playing all the games in the games room. It was only me and one or two of my friends playing pool. It was like our own private pool hall. We would take the gold-coloured vinyl cover off the pool table, rack up the balls, chalk our cues, and start shooting pool right away.

I remember so clearly on cold winter mornings, right after a night of snowfall, looking out the west windows onto the bright, quiet street between shots. The clean, freshly fallen snow covered everything, and the sun was low in the sky to the east, still blocked by the building. It looked like twilight. There was no wind, no noise, no traffic on the residential street. I would sometimes open a window, sit on the sill, and look out. The sound of the crisp crunching snow echoed up to the second floor when someone walked by on the street. It was calm and soothing. I didn't have a care in the world.

This was the time in my life I cherished, being a teenager. I was very young, but I knew what it was, and I knew it wouldn't last. I wished it would go on forever.

The First Hustle

A Nice Sunday Afternoon

After I hung up the phone, I got dressed and left my house. I was going to walk the 10 minutes down to my buddy's condo building, as I knew I would be drinking beer and I didn't want to drive the T-Bird.

It was cold and damp as I started to walk south down the street. It started to snow a little, and the wind was picking up as I got to the school. It was overcast with no sun and I started to shiver a bit, so I pulled up the collar of my coat. I could see my breath.

I walked through the schoolyard and then onto Windermere Avenue where there was almost no traffic, which was normal for a Sunday afternoon in Swansea in the 70s. I made it to the Ormskirk stairs off Windermere that took you down to the condos, and I ran down them quickly, as I was getting cold. I should have worn a heavier coat.

The Ormskirk stairs run between a large ravine, with the 65 Southport condominium on the left/south side, and the last house of Windermere Boulevard on the right/north side. They take you down about 75 feet into the Kingsway Valley, and even when running down it takes a bit of time. The entrance to the stairs is kind of hidden, and if you didn't know exactly where they were, you'd miss them.

I got to Mitch's building which was about 100 yards from the bottom of the stairs and called up to him using the building intercom. He buzzed me in and I waited in the lobby for him to come down.

There were a lot of busybodies in that building during this time, and as I was waiting, a man whom I had never seen before came into the lobby, and then stood there for a few seconds looking at me. I looked back at him, waiting for him to say something, but he didn't say anything. He walked over to the big floor-to-ceiling picture windows that looked out onto the front driveway of the building. He had his back to me. Then, without turning around, he spoke.

There was no one else around and he wasn't looking at me, so I wasn't sure if he was speaking to me or not. He said, "Are you waiting for someone? I don't recognize you."

I didn't answer for a second. Then, I said, "Excuse me, sir? Are you speaking to me?"

He turned around to face me, and then, in a condescending manner while looking me up and down, said, "Yes, I said are you waiting for someone?" I had to stop myself from telling him that I didn't know he was speaking to me as he wasn't facing me. But I was polite and told him I was waiting for someone. "Who?" he said.

Again, I had to hold back and not tell him it was none of his business. But I was nice despite his contempt for me and told him I was waiting for a friend.

"What friend?" he said.

"My friend's name is Mitch."

"Oh, I know Mitch, nice kid. Did you already call him on the intercom?"

I think to myself, *I'm sure you do know Mitch. Does this guy think I'm a complete idiot?*

"Yes, I called him."

"Oh, okay. I'm sure he'll be right down."

At this point I had had it with this guy. "I'm sure he will," I said, in a not-so-polite tone.

"Well, you don't need to be so rude," he said, and then he turned and walked away.

Mitch had come down and I heard him say hi to the guy from around the corner where the elevators are. I laughed and told Mitch what had happened. He told me he knew the guy and how he was always getting into other people's business and to not worry about it. Mitch told me a few days later the guy had complained to Mitch's parents about our interaction and that I was rude to him, but before he did, Mitch had told his parents about it. He told me his parents laughed at the guy when he showed up at their door to complain about me, and they told him to mind his own business when it comes to their son.

We got into the elevator and went down to the basement to the pool room. Getting off the elevator, it was like entering a completely different physical atmosphere. Being in the basement, you were sealed off from the outside world. It wasn't hot, but it wasn't cold either. It wasn't humid or dry, but strangely, it did feel damp. The air was thick, like you were being enveloped. It was closed in, but not confined or stuffy. It was very quiet and if you yelled, the sound disappeared almost instantly. It was almost like speaking in a vacuum. It felt like going up quickly in an elevator before your ears pop after you swallow. But you couldn't pop your ears, they weren't plugged.

The basement was where all the condo amenities were: the pool room, ping pong room, a woodworking shop, and a swimming pool. There were no windows since it was one storey below street level, and it had that distinct, unique, 70s condo smell. It was like the chemical smell from the subway, but a smell all its own. It was sort of a mix of an antiseptic smell and something else that wasn't unpleasant but also wasn't exactly nice either. It was stronger in the basement than the rest of the building, mixed with the smell of chlorine from the swimming pool. I'm not sure where that basement condo smell came from. It could have been from the building materials used, like all the 70s shag rug used on the floors throughout the building, even on some of the walls, or the chemical smell could have been from something else. I'm really not sure.

With the exception of the pool room, the walls of the main basement hallway were exposed rough concrete, brutalist type architecture. The pool room wall facing the hallway was floor to ceiling windows, giving the room even more of a hermetically-sealed feel to it. When people walked by in the hallway while you were in the pool room, you could see them, but you couldn't hear them; there was no sound at all. It was a little creepy.

I've never been in a submarine, but this is what it must be like while submerged. It all felt very dystopian – closed, sealed, clean, quiet, and controlled. It was everything and nothing all at the same time.

We make our way through the thick, soupy air to near the end of the hall where the pool room is and there's no one else around. Mitch uses his key to unlock the door and we go in. It's cold inside and the air is clean and dry. Mitch turns the lights on and the fluorescent lighting tubes in the ceiling flicker and hum as they warm up. I hear the electric baseboard heaters kick on; it warms up fast. Only the front half of the room is floor to ceiling glass, while the back half of the room is exposed concrete.

Mitch racks the balls, chalks his cue, and breaks. I grab two beers from the small cooler we brought with us, hand one to Mitch, and go and sit in a chair against the wall away from the glass wall. I don't want anyone passing by in the hallway to see the beer.

Red in the side, blue in the end. Red in the far end, pink one bank in the side. Red in the end, and a miss on the black.

About halfway into our first game, two guys come into the pool room. They are in their late 20s or possibly early 30s. We both immediately put our beers on the ground to try to hide them, but one of them looks and laughs a little and then says, "Don't worry about the beers, guys. We don't care." We reach down and pick them up.

I have finished my beer so I walk over to the cooler to get another one.

"You guys want a beer?" Mitch says.

"No thanks, but could we play the next game when you guys are done?" the other guy asks.

"Sure," Mitch says.

"Great, thanks. You guys live here?"

This wasn't a question outsiders would ask of people in a condominium. Only people who live in the condominium ask that. People who lived there, other than Mitch, were all... how should I put this, stuck up, snobby, protective, busybodies? All of the above, I'd say. This type of, "I don't know you, you must be an outsider," sort of thing, is something I only experienced in the condominiums. But I was used to it.

"I live here," Mitch says, "This is my friend. What about you guys?"

"We're visiting for a few days."

The whole exchange is odd and I get a strange feeling from them. I don't exactly know what it is, they seem nice, but there is something not right with them. The whole questioning of if we live there is odd, since they said they are visitors. The way they speak, in a very controlled way, somehow makes me uneasy. Plus, you need a key to get into the pool room even if you are already in the building, which they clearly have, as they had used it to come inside. So, even though I'm pretty sure they are legitimately allowed, their mannerisms are still a little off-putting.

The Life of a 1970s Teenager

These guys are super clean cut, and perfectly groomed. They are both clean shaven and have short, dark, freshly cut hair, greased back and parted on the left like a couple of IBM executives from the mid-60s. Both have on nicely pressed khakis and short-sleeved shirts. One guy is wearing a light blue and red-checked shirt with a button down collar and tennis shoes. The other guy is wearing a pale yellow golf shirt and brand new, dark brown suede bucks. Both are about a decade out of date.

They are both tall and thin and in perfect condition. Not too big like football players, but you can see the muscles under their shirts, so it's clear these guys work out. I have never seen them before and from the way Mitch is speaking to them, I figure he doesn't know them either.

I think right away they are military guys, but I have never seen guys like this in real life – only on American television. They speak in a slightly different accent than we do – an American accent for sure, but I can't place it. They both speak a little differently, one with an almost southern accent he is trying to hide but can't exactly, and the other one with a slight Boston accent almost like President Kennedy, but again, only slightly. They are clearly not from here.

We finish our game and I realize they have been watching us play very closely. I think they're thinking we're better than they thought. Mitch says, "The table's all yours boys."

"Thanks, guys."

Mitch and I grab another beer and sit down on the chairs against the side wall, ready to watch them play. They rack the balls and as Yellow Golf Shirt Guy begins to break, he turns to me and says, "Hey, you guys wanna play teams?"

I look at Mitch and say, "Yeah, okay, we'll play you guys. We'll break if you want."

"No, I'll break," Yellow Golf Shirt Guy says.

I put my hands up and say, "Sure."

We're playing snooker, and this is how it's played. There are 15 red balls and 6 different coloured balls. You sink a red ball, then a coloured ball, then a red ball, and a coloured ball again,

Pool, Billiards, 8 Ball, 9 Ball, and a Hundred Bucks

and that pattern continues until all the red balls are sunk. Once you sink a red ball, it stays in the pocket and each red ball is worth one point. When you sink a coloured ball, it's pulled out of the pocket and put back into play. You don't have to sink the coloured balls in order at this point in the game; you can sink whichever coloured ball you want. Only when all the red balls have been sunk do you start to sink the coloured balls in order – yellow, green, brown, blue, pink, and finally black. The coloured balls are worth the following points – two for yellow, three for green, and so on. The coloured balls now stay in the pocket until they have all been sunk, and that's the end of the game.

Yellow Golf Shirt Guy breaks but doesn't sink any balls. Mitch starts shooting and racks up a little over 10 points after about four or five shots, then misses on the black ball. Tennis Shoes Guy is up and he leans down to line up a shot but stops and stands back up. He looks over at us and says, "You guys are pretty good. Wanna make it a little more interesting?"

Mitch and I look at each other and I say, "How so?"

"Well, you wanna play for money?"

Now I know what's going on. Now I know what these guys are. Now I know why they're giving me bad vibes. These guys are a couple of hustlers! And they're going to try to take a couple of kids! Ha! They think they're better than us and that we're easy marks.

I look right at Tennis Shoes Guy and I say, "Ya, we'll play you for money, how much?" I look over at Mitch and he's looking at me a little surprised. I give him a quick wink and whisper, "Don't worry, Mitch, it'll be fun!" I look back at Tennis Shoes Guy and say again, "How much?"

"How about 5 bucks a game?" he says to me.

"Five bucks then, good." I put my hands out and say, "Continue."

As we play, I realize these guys are not very good pool players, not the worst, but not very good. I've seen guys try to hide how good they are at a pool hall. It's difficult to trick an experienced player with that sort of thing, and I don't see that here. Maybe we've met our match, but I don't think so. They've seen us play and we weren't trying to hide how good we are. We weren't trying to hustle them at all; we were playing straight up pool. Maybe they're not hustlers at all. Maybe they're stupid and think they can still beat us. These guys are hard to read.

The first game continues. We get through it quickly and we lose, but barely.

"Another game?" Tennis Shoes Guy says.

I'm having fun, so I say, "Sure."

"Double or nothing for you guys so you can even up?"

Mitch jumps up and says, "No, let's play 10 bucks a game!" and slaps his hands together.

I look at Mitch, confused for a second, as he was a little hesitant to play for the 5 bucks when I agreed to play for money earlier. I don't want to lose another 10 bucks on top of the five we're already down. So I tell the Americans to wait for a sec while I speak to my partner.

We move into the far corner out of earshot and I ask Mitch what he's doing. He says, "Let's hustle these guys."

"What?" I say, "Are you nuts?"

"Let's lose another game; then we'll up the stakes, clear the table the third game, and take them for 20 or 30 bucks."

I quickly do the math and say to Mitch, "If we lose the next game, we're down 15 bucks. If you want to take them for 30, the last game will have to be a $50 game. You sure they'll go for that?"

Mitch says, "I don't know, but it's only 15 bucks if they don't."

"What if they say they won't play for 50, like only 25?"

"I'll tell them no. It has to be worth our while to play again. It's as simple as that!"

I didn't mind playing for a little money at first, but this is different, and that's what I tell Mitch.

"Look," Mitch says, "These guys are trying to hustle us. We're better than them. We can beat them. I wanna beat them."

I think for a bit, then ask Mitch, "Are you sure you want to do this? What happens if we lose the third game? We don't even have enough money to pay them off."

"We won't lose."

"What if we do?!"

"Don't worry, I'll cover the loss. But I won't have to."

I pause and say, "Sheesh, okay. So we'll ditch the double or nothing stuff, and go with straight money games, upping the stakes as we go."

For some strange reason, I always gave in to Mitch's hare-brained schemes. That trait of mine would prove to be very dangerous a week later, for both of us.

We return to the table, and I say, "10 bucks a game okay with you guys?"

They both say "Yeah," at the same time.

We rack up the red balls and put the coloured balls in their spots on the table. Mitch breaks, sinks two reds, and then does a short run, sinking the blue and yellow. One of the Americans is up and he does pretty well too, and then misses a little short of tying up the score.

I'm up and miss on my first shot. Mitch gives me an approving look, but I wasn't trying to miss. On Mitch's next turn he sinks a red, and then sinks the white in the corner. Ha, I think, that was a pretty good fake scratch, couldn't have done better myself.

I'm playing badly and missing a lot of easy shots. I'm not trying to do that and though I'm warmed up, I'm a little nervous, and I never get nervous. The Americans aren't doing much better, so Mitch is letting them catch up. They do, and as the game progresses, they have a few good short runs, then a good run near the end putting them ahead by a safe margin. Mitch is much better at making fake misses look real than I am, and the Americans take the second game.

The last game is uneventful, but slower. There is some talk of the $50 game, and the Americans look to have doubts. But Mitch lays it on the line to them in a matter of fact but calm way reminding them that they are currently up $15. He tells them that it needs to be worth our while to play again. Tennis Shoes Guy says that he would like to keep it to a double or nothing game. Mitch says, "No, we'll take the $15 loss. But thanks anyway." Tennis Shoes Guy looks over at his partner, and they both nod. "We'll do the $50 game," he says to Mitch.

The Americans play about as well as the previous games. There is a risk they will run the table on us, and I do have concerns about that. I play better this game, and Mitch keeps it all together; we have command of the game. No need to run the table, which I think isn't a good thing to do anyway; it's a last resort if we think we are possibly at risk of losing. That isn't happening, and we continue on, playing it close. It's best to let the Americans think they lost fair and square. Every time there is a possibility of us getting too far behind, Mitch sets it straight by sinking high value coloured balls. In the end, we win the $50 game by more than 10 points.

The Americans ask if we want to play more. "No," I say, "we're done. We've been here for a while now. Good games, guys. We'll see ya."

They pay us and we leave. We took them for $35. Walking down the hallway to the elevators, I look back and see through the floor to ceiling glass walls of the pool room that the Americans have started to rack the balls again for another game. They have no idea what just happened; I mean, I don't think they do.

To this day, I don't know what the motivation was for these guys. They must have known they couldn't beat us. Or maybe, maybe, they could have swept the floor with us and were good at hiding that, better than I've seen before. Could be, but why? Well, I've thought about this on occasion over the years, and maybe they were being a couple of nice guys, giving a couple of kids some free money and in the process also giving a couple of kids a bit of a confidence boost. I guess I'll never know what they were doing, or thinking, or why. All I know, is that it was one of the oddest experiences I've ever had.

The Protocol

The next weekend, Mitch calls me on Saturday afternoon.
   "You'll never guess what's on TV tonight."
   "I have no idea."
   "The Hustler."
   "I've never seen it."
   "Come tonight and we'll watch it. My parents are going out."
   After dinner that night, I hop into the '62 T-Bird I bought the month before at the end of September – my first car. I paid $600 for it. I was 15 at the time, but I drove that car all over the city for a full year with no driver's licence and never got caught.
   In the 70s, you didn't need to have a driver's licence to own a car, or to put a car in your name. You also didn't need to have a driver's licence to get insurance for the car. And to put licence plates on the car, all you needed was to have it safety certified and have insurance. So I did all that. Though I did break the law by driving without a licence, the car was legally in my name.
   Also, in the 70s there was something nicknamed Mickey Mouse insurance. It was government insurance. It had no comprehensive coverage – meaning fire and theft – and no collision coverage. All it had was liability coverage, which was all you needed to legally drive your car at the time. It cost $50 a year, I believe, and I'm pretty sure that, to this day, this is all you need to drive legally. What I mean is, no comprehensive coverage and no collision coverage, but that type of government insurance no longer exists in Ontario.
   I drove carefully for the most part and I never got pulled over during the year before I got my driver's licence. My parents knew I was driving the car without a licence and they didn't care. I don't remember even having a conversation with them about it.
   Times were different then. From what I remember, even the cops didn't care much. If you had plates and insurance, they would fine you and warn you to take the car home and not drive

it again until you got your driver's licence. Sometimes they wouldn't even fine you.

If there's one thing I've learned, among many others, it's that sometimes it's difficult to judge the past from our current time. Although it sounds crazy now that the cops or my parents didn't care much about someone driving a car at 15 without a licence, at the time it wasn't a big deal. This detail I remember clearly.

Here's a little personal insight into my thought patterns at the time. I didn't drive without a licence only because my parents and the cops didn't care; it was the way I thought about the situation, and it was pretty much the prevalent view then. I'm sure not everyone thought that way then; that was how *I* thought. For this one thing I did back then, I take responsibility. I don't blame the police or my parents for my having driven without a licence. I did that on my own.

I drive down to Mitch's place and get there a bit after 7:30. Mitch opens the door, and as I'm walking in, Mitch's parents are walking out.

I say hi to them, and then Mitch's mom says, "So I heard you boys are going to watch *The Hustler* on TV tonight."

"Ya, I've never seen it. I heard it was good."

"Well, I know you boys like pool, so you're in for a treat. Don't forget to take the dog out, Mitch," she yells over her shoulder as she and Mitch's dad walk to the elevator. I throw my coat into the corner of the little foyer and Mitch and I walk into the big main living room of the apartment. The film doesn't start for a few minutes and Mitch gets us a couple of beers from the kitchen. We sit on the couch and have a little small talk about the movie, and then the film starts on the TV.

About a quarter of the way through the movie, Mitch looks over at me and says, "We should do that."

"Do what?" I say.

"We should go to a pool hall and hustle some guys."

"What, are you nuts? I'm not doing that!"

"Wait a sec, we could make some money here."

"How much?"

"A couple hundred bucks."

"I don't know. I don't like it. I don't think I wanna do that."

"We did it last weekend!"

"That was different. Those were just some guys from the building who thought they were hot shit and were looking to take a couple of kids."

"Yeah, but we took them."

"I know, but a real pool hall? Ever been in a real pool hall? I have. It's not what you think. It's like this movie, a lot of bad guys in there."

"Bullshit! We can take anyone."

"That's not what I'm saying. I think we could take almost anyone. It's what might happen after that I'm worried about."

"Look, we can make 200 bucks. If anything happens, we run."

"I don't know."

"Look, we've been playing for five years now, no one can beat us."

I tell Mitch maybe, and he's ecstatic. We go through an overview of some of his ideas, and I've gotta hand it to Mitch, he has it all down pat and must have had this running through his head before I even came over. I ask him and he says of course, he's been thinking about it all week. I shake my head. What can I do? I know I can say no, but I tell him I'll do it, and he smiles and starts to rub his hands together.

The movie still has a lot of time left and Mitch goes into the kitchen and then comes back with a couple more cans of beer. He hands me one and I tell him I have the car. He says, "So what? Leave it and get it tomorrow." I shake my head, take the beer, and we watch more of the movie.

Mitch's parents had a different culture when it came to beer, so it was no problem for Mitch to drink it at times. Well, anytime he wanted, actually. I asked him about that once and he looked at me funny and said, "My mom's German!" like I should have known people from Germany let their kids drink beer. I didn't.

So we have another beer, then Mitch wants to lay it all out in more detail. He gets a pad and a pencil and starts to write out a list. While writing, he says, "We'll call it... The Hustler Protocol."

"You're an idiot," I tell him.

He laughs, hops off the couch, and says he's got to take the dog out.

When he gets back from walking the dog, he picks up the pad and starts writing again as we talk about what is needed. We thought this is how you would go about hustling people.

The Following are the points we came up with:

Protocol Points

1. Draw in the marks
We start out playing 9 Ball. Few people know what 9 Ball is, and if they do, they're experienced pool players. These are the type of guys who would most likely want to play for money.

2. Get them on the hook
We act innocent. We don't play for money, we play for fun. But it would be fun to play for money, and we don't mind if the marks want to play for a little money. But we make it clear it has to be only a small amount to make the game a little more interesting.

3. Keep them in the hustle
This isn't easy. But we talk about it and come to the conclusion that the best way to keep the marks in the hustle is to act like our good shots are plain luck. We need to miss some shots by cutting the ball a little off. This will give the marks confidence that they are better than us and that they can win. The danger here is that the marks might be doing the same thing to us if they're hustlers too. We'll have to pay close attention to that, but it shouldn't be too difficult to notice this.

4. Lose a game or two

We don't want to be in the pool hall for long. We want to win some money, and then leave as quickly as we can before we are found out. We'll keep the number of games to a minimum, lose a game or two, and when we win, we make it look like we won by accident. Make the marks think they can beat us the next game when the stakes are higher. When the stakes have gotten big enough, we run the table, take the money, and leave immediately. It's not easy to do, but it's the best way to cut down on the time we're at risk.

5. How and when to end the hustle

This will be the most difficult part of the hustle. We need to take as much money as we can from the marks, but we have to be cautious. We have to evaluate when it's time to leave the game while it's happening, in real time. Even if the marks want to keep playing, we can't get greedy. That would tip them off to what we're doing. We are looking for a maximum of $200. We can end the game early if it looks like the marks are on to us, but if things are going well, we stay to the end.

6. Time to stop

When it's time to stop, we do it quickly. We don't want too much talk or argument. We say thanks and tell them we have to go. Then we take the stake money and walk out the door. We don't give the marks any warning about this; we don't want to give them any time to think about what happened. The best outcome is by the time the marks realize they got taken, if they even do, we're gone.

7. How to get out

We're only going to hustle once, meaning we'll only play teams and only with one set of guys. If things don't go well, either during the game, after the game, or when we try to leave, we run!

It was all simple and straightforward. Was it too simple? At the time we didn't think so. Heck, we were only 15, but we thought it was genius. Would it work? Again, we thought so. We were overly confident, that was for sure.

We go through every point in detail, keeping in mind anything that could mess us up, like letting the marks find out what we were really doing at any time during the game. We did know that could happen. The protocol wasn't very sophisticated but it didn't need to be. We felt it didn't matter anyway. The fallback was always to run!

The Pool Hall Hustle

It's now the next Friday. I had only worked a half day as I had worked some overtime that week, so I left downtown at 1:00 p.m., taking the subway home. I only drove to work a few days a week, parking in downtown Toronto was expensive, and it cost a lot of money for gas to feed my T-Bird's big engine.

I got home, had something to eat, and changed into some fresh clothes. It was unusually warm for the beginning of November, but my car had been sitting all night and day, so I knew it would be a little rough starting.

I fired up the T-Bird and the old girl shook a little. I sat waiting for her to settle down and thought about the night ahead and how Mitch had told me not to worry. "We're gonna come out ahead," he said when we talked about it that past Saturday. To tell you the truth, it wasn't the money I was concerned about.

I pulled out into the street on Lavinia Avenue and the power steering was loose but smooth as butter. You had to be very careful with the steering on the T-Bird. It didn't automatically return to straight after turning the wheel. Making a left or right turn meant turning the wheel back or the car would continue in the same direction you turned. If you didn't swing the wheel back straight, you would end up in oncoming traffic or on the sidewalk. I made my way down Windermere to Mitch's place.

It was late afternoon when I got to Mitch's. We had planned to hang out at his place for a while before we went to the pool hall, and his parents had gone to their cottage the day before so we would have the place to ourselves. We had a few hours to talk about the evening ahead but I wanted to relax a little before we went to the pool hall. We listened to some music and smoked on his balcony and talked about our plan briefly. Mitch wanted to talk about it more, but I shut him down. Mitch asks if I want a beer, and I tell him no, I want to keep my head clear.

By the time we were ready to go, the temperature had dropped a bit, but it was still warm as we got into the car and drove to the pool hall. On the drive there, we went over what we were going to do one last time, as we had no experience doing this. We needed that laid out plan we made the week before that detailed what could happen, and how we were going to deal with it all, fresh in our minds.

We went over again how we planned to draw our marks in, how we were going to get them on the hook, and how we were going to keep them in the hustle, as well as how and when to know it was time to end the hustle and get out.

On the point of what we were going to do if we got into any kind of real trouble, we both said at the same time, "We run!"

At 15 years old, we were both smart and mature enough to pull it off. But at the same time, we weren't old enough and were too naive to know the real risks involved. We had a lot of confidence in our ability to play a good game of pool, and both Mitch and I had cleared a table more than once. But we romanticized what we were about to do. Everything together was setting us up for a bad night if we weren't careful and things went south for us. If something happened that we either didn't prepare for, or weren't anticipating, it could put us in real danger.

We did talk about some of this a little on the drive over and decided we could handle anything that came up. Of course, that was wrong, very wrong.

We make it to Royal York Road and Bloor Street and I park the car in a laneway that runs east and west north of Bloor. There are parking spots with parking meters that run the length of the laneway from Royal York to the next street east. I park about 20 spots in, about half the length of the laneway facing north, but on an angle towards the east end of the lane. I make sure to not pull the car too far into the spot and also into about a third of the next spot over. As long as no other cars park near us, we can leave in a hurry if we have to. This way, I can do a tight swing of the wheel and drive away without backing up. I don't pay.

We start to walk the short distance over to the pool hall and Mitch says to me, "Don't you have to be 18 to be in a pool hall?"

"You're bringing that up now?" I say.

"I just thought about it. Aren't they gonna ask?"

"Yeah, they'll ask. I've got that covered, I've been here before."

"Covered how?"

"You'll see."

We walk up the stairs to the top floor where the tables are, then open the door and step inside. We both stop for about 30 seconds and have a good look around. There's no music playing and it's not busy. You can hear a few girls laughing as they play with whom I'm guessing are their boyfriends or dates about four tables into the hall, and the clacking of balls from the other occupied tables. There are a few empty tables near the door and I tell Mitch we want one of those tables.

We go to the cage to pay and the guy inside says, "How old are you guys?"

"Eighteen," I say.

"You guys aren't 18. You're not allowed to play here. If you wanna play here, you're gonna have to show me some ID."

"We'll pay double for the table," I say. The guy looks at us, then tells us the price and I pay him double. We get a set of Boston balls and take the second table from the door. The guy in the cage turns on the overhead table lights. We pick a couple of cues from a rack on the wall and check them for straightness by rolling them back and forth on the table. Mitch is happy with his, but the first one I pick isn't very straight, or heavy enough for me, so

Pool, Billiards, 8 Ball, 9 Ball, and a Hundred Bucks

I check the rack again. There aren't too many heavy cues in the rack, but I manage to find a good one.

Mitch racks the balls and I break. We start out with a few quick games of 9 Ball to try to flush out some hustlers. We don't want to take honest people; honest people wouldn't play for the kind of money we want to play for anyway. Anyone who comes up asking to play for our kind of money will probably be hustlers who know the game of 9 Ball. They will be our marks.

We play a little like we're amateurs to get the attention of anyone who might think they can take us. All of this is part of our teenage romanticized plan.

We're almost finished with our second game when a couple of older guys – I'd say they were in their early to mid-20s – from two tables over, who I see have been watching us, go up to get a couple of new cues. On their way back, they stop and ask if we want to play a few games with them. Ha! Who gets new cues after you've been playing for a while in a pool hall? We have our marks! I look up from the table and say, "Sure."

"Teams?" they say.

Mitch says, "Ya, it's getting a little boring over here. You guys play for money?"

"Sure." The big one says, "$10 a game?"

These are our marks for sure.

"We've only got $20. If we lose two games, we're scratched," I say.

"Tell ya what, we'll spot you boys 10 points, and we'll play snooker. That'll give you guys a fighting chance."

"Okay, but you break."

"We're okay with that. You boys know how to play snooker right?"

"We've played a little snooker before."

"Okay, so, snooker it is."

The little guy breaks and doesn't sink anything, and the table is pretty open. I'm up and I miss after a pretty good run: a few blues, a pink, and a brown ball. Plus we have the 10 point spot.

Now, being the smart ass I am, I say, "I didn't leave you much," which is true. This was a direct quote from the movie, *The Hustler*. Mitch looks at me, not too happy.

The tall one looks me dead in the eye and says, "You left enough." Right there, I know we might have a problem. He knows my quote and responded in kind. These guys are hustlers, straight up! But now the situation has changed. They now know that we know they're hustlers. And, they know that we know that they know we're hustlers. We are young, and I'm pretty sure they think we're suckers and that we're out of our league. What they don't know is, we are better; I've been watching them play, but we do have our work cut out for us. What we don't know is what real, possible danger we are in. We are kids playing in an adult world.

The game continues and the big one misses on his first shot and leaves Mitch wide open for some high scoring balls, which he takes full advantage of. He leaves the hustlers with not enough to win the game even if they run the table, which they don't. The little guy misses his first shot too, and I finish off the table to win the game. We're up $10 on the first game.

"Are we done, or you guys wanna play another game?" I ask.

The big one says, "Tell ya what, boys, you're both real good."

"We got lucky, we never play this good."

"Well, just so, give us a chance to make our money back. Let's up the stakes to a $25 game. 8 Ball. One game to get our money back."

"That's more than double what's in the pot right now, and almost all the money we have. You're only down 10 bucks," I say.

"Yeah, but if your luck holds out, you guys will be walking outta here with what? You'll be 35 bucks richer!"

"I need to speak with my partner."

"Of course, of course, take all the time you want."

I take Mitch aside and tell him we've got 'em on the hook, and I think we should keep 'em in the hustle. Mitch agrees, but tells me he wants $200 out of all this. I agree and tell him we play it cool and barely win. That way we might be able to keep them on

Pool, Billiards, 8 Ball, 9 Ball, and a Hundred Bucks

the hook longer and go for a few double or nothing games. If we play it right, it could net us that cool $200. We walk back over and I say, "We'll do the $25 for one more game, your choice of game."

"I said we'll play 8 Ball."

"Oh, yeah, I forgot. Rack up the Boston balls, Mitch."

As an aside, technically billiards is a specific game played with only three balls, but the colloquial term when using the word billiards, means snooker. For us Swansea boys, the terms are interchangeable.

The little guy breaks again, sinks nothing, and leaves the table open once more. Like the first guys from Mitch's condo, I'm thinking these guys aren't as good as they think they are, but I don't know. I can't figure out what their game is here. They're pretty crappy players, but they have a lot of confidence. Anyway, I sink four balls then I miss. The big guy is up and he has a pretty good run, leaving only a few balls before he can make an attempt on the 8 ball before he misses. The game is going quickly and Mitch sinks our last four balls, and on his last shot he misses on the 8 ball. Fuck, the little guy could easily pocket their last few balls then sink the 8 ball for the win, leaving us with no money. But to our surprise, the little guy only sinks two balls, leaving the 8 ball for Mitch to pocket for the win, which he does. The game is over and there's $50 in the end pocket that's ours.

Once again, I ask the guys if they're done. The big guy comes right up into my space and says, "You guys are a couple of pool hustlers."

I calmly respond with, "No, we're just a couple of kids who like to shoot pool. We're sorry you lost, but I think we're done here." Mitch knows the game is up and gets the $50 stake money from the end pocket.

"Hold on, hold on a minute," the big guy says. "Okay, maybe you guys did get lucky. Let's play one more double or nothing game."

Everything is happening so fast now. I'm not nervous, but I am getting a little confused about the money. So I say, "You mean we play for double what's in the pot, or double what you've lost?"

"Double what we've lost."

Still having trouble keeping track of the money in my head, I say, "That's a $50 game for you, are you sure?"

He looks over at his buddy and says, "We're sure."

"To be clear, if you win, we give you back $25, and you're even. If we win, you give us another $50? Is that right?"

"Yes, that's right."

"Well. Okay then. What's it gonna be, boys? Straight pool, eh? Billiards, 8 Ball, 9 Ball, and a hundred bucks?"

"50 bucks!" he says.

"Oh, yeah, right, okay," I say.

"We'll keep it 8 Ball," the little one says.

I can't believe they want to play again. If we win this game, we'll be up $85 on the night. Not as much as we were looking for after three games, but I'm starting to get a little concerned; I don't want to play anymore. I no longer care about the money. I just want to get out of there. I can tell by the way Mitch has been looking at me, he wants to leave too. These guys don't like losing, and that worries me. I look around for a quick exit for when we win. I look over at Mitch and he nods his head once okay, about playing for the $50.

"Alright," I say. "My partner says okay. But it'll be the last game." Then nodding my head I say, "We'll play 8 Ball."

We rack up the balls for the final game and Mitch breaks. He sinks two balls off the first break, then one more before a miss. The big guy comes up and misses his first shot. I come up, play well, and I clear the table and sink the 8 ball. The game is over in a matter of minutes and there's $75 in the pocket now.

The Chase

After I sink that last ball, I start to walk over to the pocket where the stake money is. The big guy is at the far end of the table, and he bends over and puts both his hands on the table felt, shoulder width apart and head down.

With his hands still on the table, he raises his head and says, "You guys are a couple of hustlers, that's for sure."

I've had it with these two guys. "So are you!" I yell across the table at him.

"Yeah, but you're better. You're a lot better."

I can see it in his eyes, he isn't fooling around. He's angry. We are in trouble.

"Look, you guys lost, fair and square," I say.

I then look over at Mitch. It's time to go. He nods to the pocket where the stake money is, then moves his head sideways towards the door. I nod and throw my cue onto the now empty table. I reach down and grab the money from the end pocket, stuff the cash into my pants pocket, and we both turn and run for the exit.

I don't know how it happened, but about halfway to the door there's a strong tug on my jacket from behind and I'm pulled down to the floor. I look up and it's the little guy standing over me, with Mitch right behind him. I must have misjudged how close he was. I don't know how he got between me and Mitch, I was paying attention to the big guy. But there he was. Mitch whacks him in the lower back pretty hard with the thick end of his cue and he's bent over in pain. I look at Mitch and he motions to the door again. I put my hands up and he reaches down and pulls me up off the floor.

The next thing I remember, I'm at the door at the top of the stairs and I look back to see where Mitch is. He is close and I see him throw his cue to the floor. In all the confusion, I don't know how Mitch got so far behind me. At the same time I see the little guy is up and both hustlers are now coming for us, but they're getting caught up by some people who are in their way after all the commotion. This slows them down a bit and buys us a little time, only a few seconds, but it's enough. We run down the stairs, and with me in front and holding the door open, Mitch trips on the last few stairs and rolls out into the street.

He quickly gets up and we run as fast as we can, with Mitch limping all the way the 75, maybe 100 yards east along Bloor. Then we turn north on Royal York and run the short distance to the lane where the T-Bird is parked, with the two hustlers in hot pursuit.

To my amazement, we make it to the car. Panting and out of breath with our hearts pounding, we both open our doors. We pause and look back, but there is no one chasing us. I look over the roof of the car at Mitch before he gets in and say, "Well, so much for the hustler protocol."

"It'll work better next time," Mitch says.

"Next time? There isn't going to be a next time. I'm never doing that again."

He looks at me, winks, and says, "Never? We'll talk about it."

I'm about to call Mitch an asshole, but before I can, he looks over the roof of the car and says, "Oh shit, here they come."

I turn and see the two hustlers hitting the edge of the laneway. "Get in, get in!" I yell to Mitch.

We both jump into the old car, Mitch yelling, "Go, go, go!" The ignition is to the left of the wheel on the dash, and in my frenzy to get out of there, I struggle a little to get the key in. Never one to let me down, she comes to life in seconds, and the smell of carbureted gasoline floods the passenger compartment. I drop her into low gear with a loud clunk, swing the wheel hard to the right, and kick the pedal to the floor. The hustlers pound their fists hard on the trunk lid as we blast down, and out of the laneway with the big T-Bird V8 engine screaming into the street. Laughing as the screeching tires burn and smoke rises into the air behind us; we leave the hustlers in a cloud of dust.

We hit Bloor Street; I push the 8-track of Boston into the stereo, and crank the volume to 8... Foreplay/Long Time! With the lead guitar kicking in, I push the gas pedal further and watch the speedometer sweep past 50 mph. We both sink down into the deep leather bucket seats and light up a smoke. There is no traffic. Within a minute we're flying across the Humber River Bridge, east, back into Swansea. We got away. And we got the money. I never stepped into a pool hall again after that day.

Me at age 14, spring 1977, skipping high school with my truant friends. Photo booth at Union Station Toronto.

Morningside Ave looking east towards Beresford Ave. Rennie Park and the Corner Bench on the right, 1978. Photo Courtesy of Ursula Fey.

My 1962 T-Bird in front of my childhood home. 85 Lavinia Ave, winter 1978.

Another shot of the '62 T-Bird, same day.

My T-Bird, "Down The Back" of 85 Lavinia Ave. My brother's '67 Camaro in "The Grave" on the right. Spring 1979. Laneway in the background leads to Durie Street.

My brother Mike's '58 Vette, the day he brought it home, Down The Back of 85 Lavinia Ave. My T-Bird on the left. It broke down on him twice on the way home. It leaked like crazy and it was raining, so he was soaked when he got home. Spring 1978.

Me on the right in overalls with a teenage friend, age 16. Fall 1978 in front of The Swansea Rec Centre, Toronto.

Me – in the middle – holding court at my childhood home in Swansea, 85 Lavinia Ave. Winter 1979, age 16.

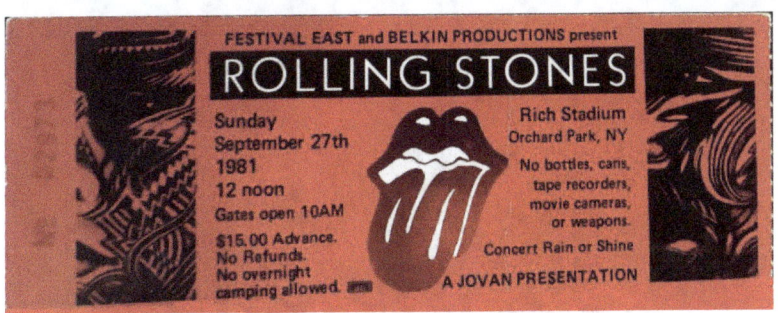

Rolling Stones concert ticket. Sept 27, 1981 near Buffalo, (Orchard Park, NY.)

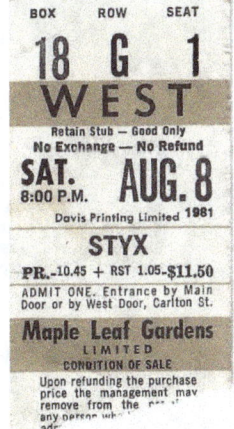

Rock Concert ticket stubs of my youth/teenage years.

December 1974. My brother Kim, age 20, with girlfriend Debbie. In front of 85 Lavinia Ave, looking north, Toronto. That is his '74 Gremlin in the background to the left. Photo Courtesy of Cathy Lovering.

Iconic Swansea Coochie Dome in Rennie Park, Toronto. Summer 2022.

My girlfriend/future wife Nancy. Summer 1980, age 18. In the back yard of her childhood home, 51 Morningside Ave, Toronto.

Me with my Les Paul Guitar in the basement of my childhood home, 85 Lavinia Ave. December 1980, age 18.

That Creepy Old T-Bird

One warm August day in 1978, I took the subway to work downtown instead of driving the T-Bird. I couldn't always afford the gas the big V8 took to drive downtown and back every day, so on occasion I wouldn't drive to work. I was 15, but I drove all over the city with no licence. I was a good driver, drove downtown a lot, and I didn't care if I got caught. I mean, I didn't want to get caught driving without a licence, but it wouldn't have been a big deal to me. I arrived home from work a little early and my mom was lying on the couch not looking too well. No one else was home. I asked her if she was okay, and she told me this story:

She had gone down to the back of our house at 85 Lavinia Avenue, where the T-Bird was parked in the back yard driveway, and there was something in the car she wanted to get. I can't remember what it was, but she had to get into the car. She couldn't just reach in through the window as whatever it was, was in the back seat and the windows were up.

The car was a two-door, and the locks on both doors were busted and never worked, so you couldn't lock the car. She got into the driver's seat and left the door wide open and then reached into the back seat. As she was reaching into the back, and fully in the car, the door suddenly, violently slammed shut all on its own. She tried to open the door, but it was locked. She tried the passenger door, but it was locked too; she couldn't get out.

It wasn't very hot, but the car was in the sun, and it was midday. She tried and tried, but the doors wouldn't open. The car had power windows, but she had no key and the car needed to be running for the power windows to work. It was getting hotter and hotter inside the car as time passed. She yelled and yelled for someone to help her, but no one heard her, and no one came.

A few hours went by, and she tried to yell again. She was getting exhausted, overheated, and dehydrated while having a difficult time breathing. Just then a Swansea boy heard her muffled calls for help as he was walking through the laneway that led out to Durie Street. He walked up the driveway from the lane to see what he was hearing, and to his astonishment, he saw my mom in the car almost passed out. He opened the door without a problem and pulled her out. He then helped her upstairs to the house and left.

After I spoke to my mom about what had happened, I went down the back and checked both doors with the windows down, and when they closed, I couldn't get them to lock. Nothing like that had ever happened before or again during the year and a half I owned that car. When I got the locks fixed a few weeks later, I asked my mechanic to check if there was any way the doors could lock on their own before he replaced them. He told me he checked and the old locks were rusted and seized open. It was impossible for the doors to lock, let alone lock on their own.

I should have sold the old girl right then. But she had been through so much with me since I owned her and had gotten me out of more than a few sticky situations, I just couldn't let her go.

In early spring of the next year, the rust and repairs were getting to be too much to handle, and I didn't have the money to fix her anymore. I also didn't want the car to sit in the grassy corner of the back yard in an area we called "The Grave," for months on end. The Grave was where the Bueler boys would put cars before they were scrapped/towed away or sold. If your car was in The Grave, it was not long for this world. The last car I remember being in the Grave was my brother's '67 Camaro with a 327 4 speed. So, with a heavy heart, I sold her.

Nothing strange ever happened again with that old creepy T-Bird. But then again, no one else ever drove it or got into the driver's seat but me.

Postscript

Creepy Old T-Bird Explanation

After writing this story, I started to think about what might have happened with the T-Bird that day.

The driveway in my back yard did have a slight grade to it. The car was parked with the front facing the top of the grade. The T-Bird was a two-door and those doors were heavy. Along with the locks, the hinges were rusted and a little seized. This would allow the driver's side door to remain open, but if you got into the car and moved around, that might be enough for the heavy door to slam shut.

As to why the doors locked, I have no explanation. The mechanic did tell me it was impossible for them to lock due to the locks being rusted and seized. It could be my mom somehow got confused and thought the doors were locked, when in fact they weren't locked and could be opened from the inside. Or she wasn't pushing hard enough for the big heavy doors to open while on the grade of the driveway.

I believe the doors were not locked, as is apparent when the boy who came to help my mom didn't have a problem opening the door from the outside.

The World
Of a 70s Teenager

Being a teenager in the 70s was great for most people, but for me, it was more than that. After I turned 16 in the fall of 1978, I was in full flight. The world was my own. I was a 70s teenager, and I was good at it. There was lots of time to be young, I knew it, and I used that knowledge to live life to the fullest.

I had a job, I had money, I had a French girlfriend, and I had fun. I had almost no obligations or any real responsibilities; plus I could drive, drink beer, work, and spend my money any way I wanted. Living at home, I didn't have to pay rent, a mortgage, or any bills. I was free to do what I wanted, when I wanted, and I did exactly that. If I didn't want to go to work one day, I wouldn't. If I wanted to stay at home and sleep all day, I did. If I wanted to stay out all night on a weekend, I did that too. I would give anything to go back, but alas, in the end, we are all prisoners of time, aren't we?

I didn't truly know how lucky I was at the time. I was happy, but I also knew I was growing up. My time in this teenage paradise, the time between being a kid and being an adult, was limited. As much as I wished it could, I knew it wouldn't go on forever.

I had an idea of what the future held. I saw it all around me. The future held adulthood and all that came with it, but at that time in my life, adulthood didn't affect me. Thoughts about a job being important and a wife who relied on me with possibly kids to take care of were far away in the future.

Many times, I looked at adults with empathy: the young mother on the subway with her hands full of shopping bags, trying desperately to settle her out-of-control toddler; the obviously stressed middle-aged man in an ill-fitting suit, looking over his resume just as he's about to enter a business for a job interview, repeatedly mouthing the pertinent points to himself, with me knowing by seeing this, he needed the job badly; the empty bottles of aftershave in the small laneways downtown I sometimes walked through on my way to work in the mornings. I often thought to myself, *How did the people who drank this stuff end up here? These people were once little kids, teenagers like me, young adults full of life with their whole futures ahead of them. What happened? Why couldn't they stop the deep decline and despair they are now in?*

Those scenes, and many others of adult life I saw during my first couple of years working, weighed on me long after I witnessed them. They made me sad and I could never get them out of my head. They return to me even today, as clear as the day I saw them over 45 years ago. As a teenager, I wanted none of it.

I never saw things like that before I started working, and it stirred up feelings inside me I also had never felt: feelings of sadness, empathy, and some helplessness. Not that I hadn't felt those emotions before, but not in this way. It's difficult to describe, more intense, more serious I would say – I didn't like it. I was becoming more mature.

I continued to enjoy my life, oftentimes with feelings of guilt, wishing I could do something to help, but knowing I couldn't. What I could do was to make sure to laugh as much as I could at things that weren't that serious, and to be nice to those around me. I always tried to help where I could and to reduce others' stress. I was not always successful in that, but I did try.

Don't get me wrong, I wasn't walking around thinking like this all the time as a teenager. These are only events and/or snapshots of situations I saw and thought of back then. Thinking like that all the time would probably drive anyone mad. When I saw something or when I was by myself doing nothing and I had time to reflect, was when I thought about all of this.

All those things I thought, felt, and experienced didn't happen on a daily basis. I mean, some of it did, at different levels, but mostly my days, weeks, and months were filled with boredom and the mundane. I wished my life could be broken up with any type of excitement. Anything, please, no more nothingness. *Just anything to break up this mind numbing, painfully dull existence.* And then... Wham! Something would happen. Right in the middle of all that excitement of the moment, right when my mind couldn't possibly be anywhere else, I would stop – just for a second or two – and step out of the reality that was all around me, I would stop and I would think, *What is this, why is life like this?* The randomness of it all was so odd to me, as it is still to this very day.

I certainly didn't know everything. I made a lot of mistakes as a teenager and it took me years to correct them. I wasted a lot of time fooling around when I should have been preparing for my future, but in the end, I straightened my life out.

These stories of my teenage life are only a small part of what was happening to me at that time. I never thought about my parents much then, and these days, I don't think about what they thought when they were the age I am now. My father has passed, and I do write a little about him in those times. I sometimes ask myself how difficult it would have been for him then. He had four kids, worked a lot of hours, and had almost no time for himself. My parents were in their forties when I was a teenager. My mother is still alive, in her nineties, and lives by herself in an apartment.

Do I look ahead like I used to? No, and I don't know why. Maybe I don't wish to. I've got about all the material things I've ever wanted. I'm a pretty simple guy when it comes to that, and I don't need a lot to live happily. I have always lived modestly and have never had a desire for excess. I don't need a million-dollar Arabian horse, just give me an old paint and I'm happy. This statement sums up my take on life pretty well.

Though I was successful in my career, I never chased money. Others around me were different and gave their whole lives to their jobs. I have lost some friends over time; they couldn't accept that I didn't care so much about a lot of the things they cared about. If I didn't like something, like a job, I would walk out without looking back. I did that a lot during my teens.

Many people in my life could never understand why I don't care about things that are so important to them. Could it be they wish they could live the way I do but don't have the courage to do so? Could it be they're too afraid to drop something that makes them feel secure? I don't know the answer. I have experienced some judgment about how I live my life on occasion. But I live my life in the way I want, and if people don't like it, they should mind their own business. For the most part, I live my life one day at a time. I don't dwell on the future all that much, at least not enough to make the present, and the people around me uncomfortable.

Some have gone so far as to tell me I should be living my life the way they live theirs. When I do not agree with their suggestions or question them as to why I should live the way they do, they get angry with me. Some have even told me I'm an idiot, or think of me as such, because I'm not like them. They don't always do it in a direct way. Many times, it's been done in a passive-aggressive manner, or by talking behind my back to others. I always see right through that, and I have had to remove a lot of people from my life because of it.

I'm a lone wolf, a renegade if you will. I'm a critical thinker, and I question everything. I have always lived my life this way. I have paid a high price at times for living this way, but I sleep fine at night.

Many people like to be, or are, a member of a tribe, whatever that tribe may be. When they observe others going against societal norms, or against the tribe they think someone belongs to, or should belong to, they can't understand it, and see that person as a threat, or even as an insult to them personally.

They don't understand why the other person is not like them; they can't understand why that person is so contrary, even if it is explained to them in detail. They often have real contempt towards these people for their successes, achievements, and the happiness they themselves do not possess. They feel anger and frustration because they aren't able to get what someone else has. They can't figure out how that person got it, and they can't figure out how to get it for themselves. Sometimes these are material things, but often, it's the happiness and contentment they see, yet cannot achieve.

They project their personal dissatisfaction onto others. Their own inadequacies, and/or their own perceived or real personal failures or the unhappiness in their lives gets put on others.

What is the context here for me? Does it come from anger, bitterness, or meanness? No, not at all. It comes from the frustration of others telling me how I should live my life. If someone is unhappy in life, then only that person can change it. This means that only an individual can make themselves happy and have contentment. Looking to others for that won't happen, and judging others never will. You can't control what others do or think. All you can do is control your own reaction to things that happen in your life.

I have never lived in anger. I have always been internally happy and content with whatever comes my way. People can't understand why I am always so upbeat, even in the face of adversity, when they are not, even when they have everything one could ever want. But there is something missing in their lives. I feel the judgment coming from others comes down to that.

I'm not a Baby Boomer, and I'm not a Gen-Xer. I'm part of a group not a lot of people have heard of: Generation Jones. Demographers say Generation Jones are people who were born between 1954 and 1964, but it's between 1959 and 1964. I'm right in the middle of this. In my experience, generally, people born during this time didn't hang out with people who were born before or after these years.

We are our own generation. None of us could ever relate to Boomers or Gen-Xers. We were, and still are, very different. If you asked any one of us what defines our generation, I think they'd say we are the generation that never takes ourselves too seriously; we laugh a heck of a lot more, we're a lot calmer, and we don't care all that much about the same stuff that bothers the other generations. We do try to go with the flow. There is an old saying that pretty much sums up our outlook on life: "Things that seem urgent are seldom important. Things that are important are seldom urgent."

If there is one negatively perceived trait of my generation, it would be we don't care all that much, we're not uptight, and we don't see apathy as a negative.

My personal generational observations have more to do with culture than the economic conditions of the times. Even though economic conditions can and do drive culture to some extent, my generation in their youth was more renegade than rebel. These two words are often used, or thought of as synonyms, but they are quite different.

Times were different for my parents when they were in their prime compared to how times were when I was in the prime of my life. But were they? Working like crazy with limited sleep, worrying about the kids, the car payment, the mortgage, etc., I think there are a lot of things in life that are universal and don't change over time. I also think worrying about what is to come all the time is a fool's game. Doing that too much will eat you up.

I Don't Believe You

It was a hot Friday night in mid-July of 1979, I was 16, and I was going to meet up with the gang at Rennie Park. We were all going to hang out and do what most teenagers in the late 70s did in a park at night – drink beer.

I was running late, going for a few beers with my co-workers after work that night in downtown Toronto. I got home and changed into some fresh clothes, and then made my way down to Rennie through the back lane of my house on Lavinia Avenue, out onto Durie Street, down Morningside Avenue, past the Corner Bench at the northwest entrance, and into the park.

The Corner Bench is still there. I can't tell you how many times I sat on that bench when I was a teenager. It was sometimes the place where I sat alone in silence just reflecting, waiting for friends, or looking at the big yellow willow tree right in front of me while it moved with the wind as the warmth of the day enveloped me in summer.

In winter, I'd sit there pulling up my coat collar as the cold wind whistled all around me and made me shiver, wondering where my friends were. At other times, I'd sit there with my friends, laughing and carrying on. Sometimes deciding what we were going to do next, sometimes deciding we weren't going to do anything at all. We'd cancel our plans and just sit and enjoy each other's company right there at our special bench.

I do miss those carefree days – the days between being a child and being an adult, with almost all the privileges of adulthood without any of the responsibilities. Strangely, I did know those days would come to an end, and it all ended too soon – way too soon. Sadly, the big yellow willow tree is now gone. The tree was damaged in a heavy storm some years ago and had to be removed, but my memories of the Corner Bench remain strong. Those long days on the Corner Bench will always be with me. Reflecting, waiting, and just taking Rennie Park in as my own personal oasis; winter, spring, summer, and fall.

I start to walk through the park and it's almost dark, but I can see a couple of my buds sitting on one of the big dark green park benches under the Coochie Dome (see Appendix A), near the south end of the park. They have a beer case under the bench. If you were a teenager in the 70s in Swansea, chances are you were drinking beer in Rennie Park. Or like me, most weekends. Police cars in the 70s in Toronto were painted all yellow, and there were very few yellow private cars then, so if you were in the park and caught a glimpse of yellow, that was your quick visual cue that it was time to book it out of there!

The best escape route was up the stairs from behind the rinks, up to Ellis Avenue. Most times we would watch the cops from a distance, and then return to our beer drinking in the park once they left. We were such little stinkers. On this day, though, there were no yellow cop cars to run from, but my friends told me a story about something else they had to run from.

I make it to the Coochie Dome and sit down on the bench. One of my buds hands me a beer, and the small talk starts. "Why are you late?" and stuff like that. I tell them I went out with my co-workers and ask what's up with them.

They both look at each other and say, "Well..." and they start to tell me what had just happened to them.

They met at the Swansea School north end parking lot right before dusk, and started to walk down Waller Avenue to the park. Just as they were a few steps from the parking lot, right at the top of the school hill, they heard this strange, eerie, wavering sound all around them – an oscillating hum. They looked around, but didn't see anything. They continued down Waller and about halfway down the street, they saw something slowly coming out from, or rather flying out from, Catfish Pond marsh a little south of the park clubhouse.

The eerie, wavering sound was getting louder, and a blue light appeared over the marsh. They looked over the school field to where the light was coming from as something started flying towards them.

At this point, I look at them both and ask them how many beers have they had?

They laugh and say only a few, and continue the story. They say as it got about halfway across the school field, they saw it was some type of flying saucer. It stopped and hovered about 50 feet in the air. The saucer was about the size of a small car with red, blue, and green flashing lights. There was a strong smell of ozone in the air now, like it had just finished raining, but it hadn't rained in days.

There was no one around and by now they were both freaking out. They dropped the case of beer they had and started to run down Waller and into the park. As they ran down the street, the saucer started to move more quickly, across the field towards them. They made it to the park and ran down the grass hill; they then turned around and saw the saucer right above them.

The eerie sound had become a low-level thumping hum, and they continued to run through the park as the saucer hovered lower and chased them. They ran diagonally towards Runnymede Road and made it to the little square pathway at the far northeast corner of the park. They ran into the thick bushes at the bottom of Runnymede to hide.

The saucer caught up to them, stopped at the edge of the bushes, and hovered at the top of the tree line. It made a *whoop-whoop* sound, spun around a few times, then took off the way it came at breakneck speed.

"Then what happened?" I ask.

"Nothing, we went back and got the beer case and waited for you to get here."

"The saucer never came back?"

"Nope," they both say.
"I don't believe you!"
"Well, that's what happened."

At this point I don't know what to think, but they are both pretty shook up after telling the story. Some more of the gang show up, and they retell the story. Everyone says they don't believe them.

As the years have gone by, I have seen them both once in a while, and I've asked them about the story. Each time over all those years, they never wavered from their story; they have never laughed, smirked, or changed it. And each time I saw them and I brought up the story, they were as shook up talking about it as the night it happened.

I have no idea what happened that night, but not once in my long life have I ever seen or experienced anything supernatural or anything that didn't have a good logical explanation. Life is, and can be, very random. Sometimes we don't always see how or why things happen.

Most people are looking for meaning and purpose in life. What is our purpose? What is the meaning of life? Why are we here? My answer is there is no meaning or purpose to life. There is only the meaning and purpose we ourselves make.

For me, there is no all-knowing, all-powerful being or entity controlling everything. I believe there is only us and what we do; life, the universe, and everything in it, is a coincidence of chemistry and physics. And there is certainly no predestination. If there is not full agency over one's actions and will, how can responsibility be assigned? I have never thought differently. At the risk of sounding sanctimonious, the more people realize this, the more we will all live a happier, more fulfilling, and meaningful life, and maybe, just maybe, that realization will make a difference. The best way to do that is to try to live a moral life. How do you live a moral life without some type of outside force to guide you? This can be done through the objectivity of morals, and it all comes naturally. Help others when you can and do the right thing.

Mercury Blues

In the summer of 1979, I was 16. After selling my '62 T-Bird in the spring, l bought a four-door 1973 Mercury Montego Brougham. It was the worst colour of brown, and the ugliest car I ever owned. It seated 10 comfortably and it was loaded. It had power everything: seats, windows, steering and brakes, plus air conditioning. I paid $600 for it and by the time I got it, the windows still worked sometimes, but the other power options, not so much.

The power steering only worked once in a while, and the brakes malfunctioned to the point that when anyone else drove the car, I told them to try to not use the brakes too much. I had to use a crowbar to move the seat back and leave it in place so the seat wouldn't move forward. The crowbar would come loose sometimes while I was driving, and I would be thrust up against the steering wheel. This car had a huge 429 V8 engine and when I drove it on the highway, the gas gauge would move faster than the clock. It had been modified and fitted with a four-barrel carburetor bumping up the horsepower a bit. It was a very fast car, when you hit the gas pedal, it went.

Everything was wrong with this car, and I shouldn't have been driving it on any public road.

One time, I turned on the wipers in the rain and the horn started blaring on and off. The cops pulled me over, they thought something was wrong. I couldn't stop laughing while trying to tell them all I had done was turn on the wipers. They were not too happy with me and disconnected the horn right there in the street – no ticket, though.

I want to preface this story by mentioning drinking and driving. Although there was some of that in those days, my friends and I never did that, but I did know people who did and got caught. Though we did break the law with alcohol accessible to the driver, the cops didn't care about that too much in the 70s and I'm not even sure if that was a law back then. If it was, I don't remember it ever being brought up, by us or the police. I never drove after drinking, and I never got in a car with a driver who had been. It wasn't something we did. With all that said, here we go...

In the late 70s, my buddies and I used to cruise Yonge Street – the main drag in Toronto – during the summer weekends. One hot Saturday night in '79, we all piled into the Mercury and took off for a night of fun downtown. Jim was driving, with Rob in the front passenger seat, and James and I sat in the back. I'm pretty sure Daniel was in the back with us too. The car was so friggin' huge and there was lots of room all around.

We're all having a real hoot driving up and down Yonge Street with Max Webster blasting out of the cassette stereo.

On our third or fourth pass up and down the strip, we see cop car lights behind us. We weren't paranoid and thought nothing of it, but they were pulling us over and Jim co-operated. We were all drinking beer, but not Jim.

Two cops come up to Jim and ask for all the normal paperwork. Just then, the crowbar holding the seat back fails, and Jim is thrust into the steering wheel. The cop freaks out a bit and puts his hand on his sidearm. The cop says, "What's going on here?" and Jim explains the crowbar thing. The cop allows him to get out and fix it while they go back to their car to check out his papers. It's hot and we have all the windows open. When they return, one cop gives Jim's papers back to him.

I was on the driver's side in the back. The other cop flashes his light into the car and sees we have a case of beer on the floor in the back. All three of us in the back were drinking, and I had an open beer between my legs.

The cop shines the light down to my beer and says, "What is that?"

All I can say is, "It's a beer, sir." He gives me an angry look and I think, *Great, this is it. I'm going to friggin' jail.* He tells me to get out of the car and to bring the beer with me.

I get out of the car in front of a ton of people who are all in the street. The cop looks at me and says, "Pour that out," so I do. He then tells me to get back in the car and take the empty with me, which I do. He leans into the car and says, "Now, what is that?" while pointing to the case of beer on the floor.

All I can say is, "It's a case of beer, sir."

He looks around the car some more, then says, "You fucking kids get out of here right now and go home or you're all going to jail!"

Jim says, "Yes, sir!" then starts up the car and we leave.

If this happened now, we would all have been in cuffs and headed to jail for an overnight stay with a court appearance in the morning and the car would have been towed and/or impounded.

But that was the 70s and, of course, we went out the very next weekend and did it all over again. Just some 70s teenage shenanigans.

I had the car for about eight months before it totally fell apart, then I scrapped it. The last week I had it, the power steering started to go, then the brakes. I had trouble starting it, then when I shut it off and removed the ignition key, it would keep running. I had to remove the coil wire to stop it from running. Then it wouldn't go into reverse. It was an interesting week.

A Window with a View

August 30, 1979

Like most teenagers at the time, I spent a lot of time in my room. In the 70s, there were no iPods, no computers, and there was no internet; no digital music of any kind. All music was analog. On Sundays, a local radio station – Q107 – would play old rock music from the late 60s and early 70s all day. A lot of Sunday afternoons, I would queue up my cassette player and tape a bunch of songs, trying my best to cut out the commercials. After a while I got pretty good at it.

What I hated was when the DJ would talk over the intro to the song, except when they would "Hit the post." This meant the DJ would talk right up to the split second before the singing would start in a song. Now, this was an art form for a DJ to do correctly and his timing had to be right on, and I liked it if it was done right.

It's very late on a Thursday evening, around 2 a.m., and I'm doing some taping from the radio tonight. My room is on the second floor of our house in the front, and looks out over the street, so I can see anything that happens there. It's a hot summer night and I'm about to turn 17 in a week's time. It had been close to 90°F that day and the temperature hadn't dropped much. I'm taking a break from taping and I'm at my window having a smoke and drinking a beer, with ELO's Telephone Line playing in the background.

It's completely silent outside, when I hear a car coming up the street from the south; my house is on the east side of the street.

The Life of a 1970s Teenager

It's driving slowly and quietly, then it passes by my house. The car was a black '68 or '69 Dodge Charger. I didn't get a good look at it, but I knew what it was. After about a minute, I hear this loud screeching of tires that sounds like it's coming from about 50 yards away. Eventually, the car comes into view going really fast, in reverse, and the tires are smoking. The car passes by my house and loses control, swerves, leaves the road, and smashes into the sunken driveway of the house two doors down on the opposite side of the street. The car's engine has stopped and it's just sitting there with smoke coming from the undercarriage.

Everything is silent again, except for the sound of steam coming from the car's radiator. I'm at my window looking out at the scene in utter amazement, and I open another cold beer from the mini fridge I have in my room. I mean, what else can I do?

There is no movement from inside the car for at least a minute, and it was a very long minute. I'm just staring at the car when suddenly it starts up, and pulls out of the driveway the same way it went in. A bunch of bricks from the driveway are all coming out into the street and sparks are flying everywhere. It then races back up the street, with its tires screeching all the way.

Complete silence again. Not one person comes out of their house, and I am completely stunned at this point.

Some time passes as I'm trying to take this all in, and as I'm sitting there staring out the window, I thought I saw the passenger, and it looked like my older brother, Kim.

About 10 minutes go by, and still there is no one in the street. Eventually, I hear footsteps in the distance and they are getting closer to my house. I look out the window, but don't notice anything until I see my brother walking down the street towards our house. I back away from the window and do nothing as he comes into the house. I hear some muted talking downstairs, it's him talking to my mother. A few moments later, I see him leaving and getting into my mother's car, which is parked right in front of our house. He gets in, starts it up, and drives away, then nothing. I stay up for a while, but nothing else happens, so I go to sleep.

That Night I had a Dream

I find myself driving my brother's 1967 Camaro RS alone through the small, quiet streets of Swansea. No radio; just the wind, the thunder of the small block 327 engine, and the sound of the four speed transmission as I tear through the gears.

I stomp the pedal to the floor. The engine races as I switch into 3rd and the rear wheels screech out of control. I can smell the clutch burning. I've never felt so alive!

All of a sudden, the cops are on my tail. How do I get away? Ahhh yes, the old back lane trick. With cop lights illuminating the whole street and cop sirens awakening the whole neighbourhood, I lead them down Deforest from Windermere. As I crest the Deforest hill at Durie, I brake with all my might, and quickly gear down to 2nd. I pop the clutch, hit the gas, and crank the wheel hard to the right. The rear wheels skip and chirp as I round the corner. The rear end gets away from me as it slides to the left, but I gain control giving her more gas and she straightens out. I hit the lights, roar south down Durie, and disappear through the dark of the back lane. I reach my back yard and drive right into the open garage. The cops didn't even see me enter the lane. They have no chance of catching me.

When I see my brother the next day, I ask him what happened last night. He tells me he and a friend from work were out at a restaurant and his friend drove him home. He says his friend passed our house, but didn't realize it until they were way up the street. He then reversed down the street and crashed into the driveway. When they drove back up the street, the car wouldn't start again. So my brother walked back down the street to our house and got my mom's car to take the guy home. The next day, the guy had his car towed.

No cops ever came, and not one person on the street ever said anything to anyone, not a peep. A few weeks later, I saw some workers had come and repaired the damaged driveway. After all that, we never heard another word about it.

My '78 Gibson Les Paul

I bought this guitar in late fall of 1979 when I was 17. I have never gigged with it, only in a garage band in my teens and early 20s, so the guitar is in near mint condition. We used to play sometimes in the garage down the back of my house on Lavinia Avenue. It's true the whole neighbourhood could hear us, good and bad. We played a lot of Led Zeppelin and a lot of Rush.

I had to get a bank loan to buy it, and I paid $700 for it. It is now worth considerably more. I remember so well going to the bank to get the loan. I could not stop talking about how dependable I was with my job, and that I was making good money. I can't remember the whole conversation with the loans officer, but I couldn't stop talking. So the loan officer just cut me off and said, "Todd, it's okay. You can stop talking now. You can have the money."

Well, I was still talking, then I just stopped. "I can?" I said.

"Yes, it's fine," she said.

I was so happy. She gave me the money right there and then in cash, and I got the guitar that night. I was sweating buckets when I walked out with the cash. I'll never forget that day.

I would never sell it. Even in difficult times, it has never, not once, crossed my mind to let it go. But I will say it has been in hock at a pawn shop more than once. Such is life. I will say, though, having my baby in a hock shop for a few months was extremely stressful. I would advise against it.

The guitar has a three piece maple top, solid mahogany body, three piece maple neck, rosewood fretboard, a DiMarzio Dual

Sound (PAF) pickup in the neck position and a DiMarzio Super Distortion pickup in the bridge position, Schaller machine heads, Schaller Roller Bridge, lightweight aluminum tailpiece and tailpiece mounting stud posts, a small neck volute, a vintage toggle switch knob, some amber vintage top hat control knobs that go to 11, and it weighs nine pounds.

It sounds amazing; I've never played a guitar that has the incredible tone that this baby does. It's so heavy; you can only play it standing up for about two hours before your shoulder starts to give way. I've been playing this guitar for 45 years now, but mostly off strap. I do have a wide leather strap I used when I was a teenager in the 70s which does help with the weight on the shoulder.

This is a Norlin era guitar, meaning it was made during the time a company named Norlin owned Gibson. The guitar was made in Nashville, Tennessee in November 1978. The year 1978 was one of the highest quality years after the earlier Norlin era quality control issues. Mine is the first year of the solid body after the pancake body era. Apparently, the natural colour finish was only 1.3% of the Les Pauls made between 1970 and 1980.

I started playing guitar in the fall of 1979, when I was 17. Right away I began formal private guitar lessons that continued for a full year. I would take the subway every Saturday afternoon from Swansea up to Yonge Street and Eglinton Avenue for my one hour weekly lesson. My guitar teacher had a small studio in one of the low rise buildings on Yonge, and he would teach me Led Zeppelin, Pink Floyd, and other rock music of the day. Playing guitar has a steep learning curve, and most don't continue playing very long after starting because they become frustrated. Learning how to play that music was what made me a lifelong guitar player, as I was happy to be able to play the music I really liked, and play it correctly.

Of course I also had to learn music theory. I didn't mind though. By the time I stopped taking lessons, I could sight-read music. This helped me immensely to learn and play complicated musical arrangements before I was 20.

My '78 Gibson Les Paul

My guitar teacher had an old, beat up, '59 Gibson Standard Burst Les Paul that he would play while teaching me. I played it more than a few times at my lessons. At the time, I only thought it was a cool, old, beat up guitar. I had no idea what it was.

One day I showed up for my lesson, and my teacher had this brand new, beautiful, shiny, ebony Les Paul Standard.

I said, "Ooooo... nice guitar. What happened to your old one?"

He told me one of his older students offered him $5,000 for it, plus this brand new Standard. I had no idea then I had been playing such an iconic guitar at my lessons until years later. That 1959 Les Paul guitar would be worth over $500,000 today.

Tell Me Why I Shouldn't Take Your Licence

Drivers in Ontario, Canada start out with zero demerit points on a driver's licence. When convicted of a moving violation, depending on the offence, demerit points accumulate up to a maximum of 15 points. At that time, a licence is automatically suspended for a certain amount of time.

After almost a full year of having my licence, which I got on my 16th birthday after passing both the written and road tests on the same day, I managed to accumulate 12 demerit points; these were for speeding, rolling through stop signs, illegal left turns, and even driving the wrong way down a one-way street.

I believe at the time, after 9 demerit points, they could call you in for an interview, and take your licence. At 12 points and above, the government could suspend your licence with no interview, but that wasn't always the case. Sometimes you would be called in for an interview; this was the case for me at the time.

I finally got called in for an interview with the Ontario Ministry of Transportation. When I arrived at the meeting, they took my licence from me right away, telling me I might get it back depending on how the interview went.

The guy who interviewed me was very nice and calm. We talked about all my offences, and he asked me the details about each one. Although all the driving offences on the surface looked bad in totality, they weren't all that dangerous. The speeding was for 10 mph over. Rolling through a stop sign was just that, not running the sign outright. The illegal left turn was at a stop light where the turn was outside of the allowable day/time. Driving the wrong way on a one-way street was a stupid mistake I made when I wasn't paying attention.

Looking back on it now, I knew the interviewer understood he was talking to a kid who had made a number of mistakes in a short time but wasn't malicious. To tell you the truth, I couldn't have cared less if they had taken my licence at the time, and I wouldn't have driven afterward if they did. I didn't have a bad attitude during the interview, and I wasn't rude, argumentative, or rebellious. I didn't care what happened. I don't know why, but I was indifferent to it all.

After our little talk, he asked me, if I got caught all these times, how many other times did I break the law without getting caught? He said the police can't be everywhere all the time. I told him none, which was the truth.

He then asked me why he shouldn't take my licence right then and there. I had no answer, so I told him the truth and said I didn't know. He then asked me if I had anything else to say, and I said no.

He got up and told me to wait, then left the room, closing the door behind him. He kept me waiting alone in the room for about 20 minutes.

When he came back in, he didn't have my licence with him. I thought for sure he was going to take it. He looked at me and said in a calm and soothing voice, "Look, Todd, you seem like a nice, honest kid. I'm not going to take your licence today, but you must stop breaking the law, and start paying more attention to what you're doing. These laws are in place for a reason. If I see you in here again, that's it, I'll take your licence. You can go now and pick up your licence at the front desk."

I thanked him and left the room to get my licence. When I got to the front desk, the woman handed me back my licence and said, "He's in a good mood today, you're lucky. I've never seen anyone walk out of an interview with 12 points and get their licence back." I thanked her and left. I walked out thinking it was the first time an adult – other than my parents – believed me when I told them the truth.

After that day, in the last 45 years of driving in Toronto, I think I have had one or two small speeding tickets. I think the interview guy being so nice, understanding, and empathetic to me at the time made an impression on me. I believe he cared about me, and just wanted me to go down the straight and narrow path, which I did.

If a kid is shown others care for them, it can make a huge difference in how they conduct themselves in their adult lives. That seemingly unimportant interview and short experience in my life did make a difference for me. Maybe it wasn't so unimportant after all.

True or False
Part II

1. In the summer of 1973, Queen Elizabeth II visited Toronto. On the day she came through High Park, I was arrested, or should I say detained, after swimming at the park pool. Let's just say I was held by the police, after I ran across the street in front of her car. I had no idea it was such a big deal.

2. I still have four wisdom teeth in my mouth, and all are impacted. They have never been a real problem, so I haven't had them removed.

3. I have a deviated septum.

4. I have a rare brain tumour that only three people in one million have. I've had it since I was 14, but it doesn't affect me.

5. I ran the New York City Marathon at age 42.

See Appendix C for detailed answers.

1F2T3T4T5T

High Roller Baby

In the spring of 1980, I was 17. Going to rock concerts in the city was a regular occurrence for me at the time. I planned to go with two guys I worked with to the April Wine concert at Maple Leaf Gardens in downtown Toronto, with Johnny Winter as the opening act. I can't remember what day the concert was, but it must have been in the middle of the week, I remember going straight from work, and going back to work the next day.

Steve said he was able to get us good tickets to the show from his brother, who knew a guy, who knew a guy. Then the morning of the concert arrives and Steve shows up to work empty handed. I wanted to see April Wine that night, as it was the only show they were going to do in Toronto that year.

Hank and I are now both pretty pissed off at Steve, but Steve has an idea. "And what would that be?" I ask him.

"We can get tickets from scalpers," Steve says.

"Scalpers? I don't want tickets from scalpers. It'll be too much."

"Not always. There are usually a bunch of scalpers out on the street right at the start of the show. If we wait until after the concert starts, we can get a good deal because they have to get rid of the tickets or they'll be worthless."

I look over at Hank and he says, "Well, I mean, we could try."

"Ya, okay," I say, "I really want to see April Wine."

When five o'clock rolls around, we finish work, then go to the bar downstairs for dinner and a few beers. The concert was set to start at 7 p.m.

Steve is in his early 20s with a full moustache, and Hank is in his mid-20s with a pretty strong beard. We all have long hair, though I'm clean shaven with a young-looking face. Since I am underage, I've never gone into that bar without either Steve or Hank and have never had an issue being served.

I had been going to bars since I was 15, and for some reason whenever I went into a bar with older guys, I always got served with no questions asked, though I did sometimes get looks. If I tried to go in with guys my own age, it was always a no-go. I learned that on more than one occasion, so I stopped trying. I figured it was a social engineering thing, like most people think anyone with the correct uniform on in the right setting should legitimately be there. Most people won't question it, even if they might feel something is off. If I was with older guys, the servers thought I was of age but just looked young. I always won the Guess Your Age game at carnivals and fairs, even well into my forties.

After eating, we walked to Davisville subway station and headed south the six stops to College station, where Maple Leaf Gardens is. I remember it being mid-April.

I know this as I was still making payments on the Les Paul guitar I had bought months prior. The payment came at the first of the month and I didn't have to make a payment from this cheque.

Although I love to wear my jean jacket, even when it's cold out, this day was too cold, below freezing. So instead, I have on my blue 70s parka I've had for years, it's comfortable and warm. Steve has on his Levi's jean jacket, and he's shivering. Hank is wearing a beautiful leather motorcycle jacket with the diagonal front zipper, that coat is very warm and heavy. I had been trying to get Hank to sell me his motorcycle jacket for months. I could never afford a new one, and I figured Hank would tire of the jacket and give me a good deal on it one day, but it had always been a hard no.

A little after seven o'clock, there are still a lot of people milling about on the street outside the Gardens. There are a few cops, and I can see what looks like scalpers making last minute deals with people. As we walk by, some of them are flashing tickets at us and saying, "Tickets, who needs tickets?"

Steve approaches a scalper and asks him what he's got. "I got Reds and some Golds left," he says.

Steve says, "How much for the Golds?"

"Forty bucks," the guy says.

Now I know the ticket's face value is around ten dollars, and I say, "The concert's already started. We're not paying forty bucks."

"I'll give ya the Golds for $30."

"We'll take them for $25."

"Okay, I got four, a hundred bucks."

"We only need three."

"I can't sell you only three. They're the last four I got."

"Then we'll go to your buddy right there," and I point to another scalper about 10 feet away.

The scalper looks around for a minute, but says okay. We pay him and take the three tickets. The strange thing I notice at this point and I don't know why I didn't see it before; there are cops watching all this and they aren't doing anything about it. Scalping concert tickets was illegal then, but both the cops and the scalper aren't fazed at all about it.

We walk into the concert and cops are searching everyone. I don't have anything on me, but I know Steve has a small amount of weed in a baggie in his sock. They search me, then Hank, then Steve, but they don't check our socks. On the subway on the way down, Steve says not to worry, they never check socks. As we walk away from the cops, Steve looks over at me and smiles. I just shake my head.

We get to our seats and a couple of guys are sitting in them. The concert is pretty loud, and I can't hear Hank talking to them. But I do see Hank showing the guys his ticket and it looks like there is a little verbal exchange. Then the guys get up from the seats, leave, and Hank motions us over. There is one thing that sticks out strongly in my mind about this show; after Johnny Winter had finished his set and April Wine came on – it was the loudest concert I have ever been to.

We didn't talk to each other during the show; it was so loud, we could only manage a little chit chat between songs. The show was great and I enjoyed it, and when it ended, the members of April Wine said, "Good night, Toronto!"

The house lights don't go up, so while we wait for the encore, the crowd is rowdy and super loud. Steve says he'll be right back, gets up from his seat, makes his way through the row, and walks up the aisle stairs. I have no idea where he is going, and he doesn't come back until halfway through the first encore song, a cover of King Crimson's "21st Century Schizoid Man."

When Steve comes back, I have to scream into his ear through the unbelievably loud music, even though we are sitting right next to each other.

"Where have you been?" I ask Steve.

"I just ripped off two guys for a half ounce of pot," he says.

"What? How'd you do that?! Forget it, I don't wanna know. They better not be coming after you. I want to finish watching the encore."

"I'll tell you later."

"I'm sure you will."

"Don't worry about it. What are they gonna do, call the cops? I lost them anyway."

"I hope so," I say. Then I turn around and see two sketchy guys looking around from the top of the aisle, and they've got two cops with them.

I turn to Steve and say, "Are you sure you lost them? 'Cause I think they're right there."

Steve looks around and says, "Fuck, that's them!"

"And they've got two cops with them," I say. "Good job, Steve. Keep your head down, maybe they won't see us."

"Damn, too late," Steve says. "Here they come."

Hank asks me what's going on and I tell him the best I can. He shakes his head and stares at Steve, none too happy.

I look over and see they've spotted us and they're coming down the aisle.

Shit, I wanted to see the end of the show. "Thanks a lot, Steve," I say.

We all get up and make our way through the row past about five people, to the aisle on the other side. When we get there, I turn around and see the cops and the sketchy guys just entering the row, with the cops leading. One of the sketchy guys, the small one, turns around and goes back up the aisle, hoping to catch us on the landing, as we're running up the stairs. I have no idea why the cops tried to come through the row of people and not go back up the aisle to cut us off, but that's what was happening.

We make it to the landing where all the beer and snack stands are, which are about 25 or 30 feet from where we are. It's a little busy, but not overly. I look down the stairs where we came from and the cops are still struggling through the row of people trying to get to the aisle. I look over to the stairs where I was expecting the sketchy guy to appear, but he's only made it to his side of the aisle. Looks like we're in the clear. They won't be able to catch us before we go down the stairs on the other side of the landing.

We run over to the nearest stairway exit that will take us to street level, and as we get to the top of the stairs, I look back. The landing is much narrower here where we are, so I can easily see down the stairs on the other side from across the landing. I see the sketchy guy at the top of his aisle; he's now on the landing. He sees us and starts to run across the landing towards us. Then I turn my head and I can see down the aisle we came up as it's directly across from where we are now. I see the two cops coming up and they are getting close to the top of the stairs to the landing. One of the cops gets a good look at me. I tell all this to Steve and Hank as we run down the stairs, and Hank says, "Don't worry, I know where to go where they can't follow us."

"I hope so," I say. Hank had worked at Maple Leaf Gardens for about a year a while back and knew the layout pretty well.

We make it to street level, and Hank directs us down an out-of-the-way corridor with a sign that reads, "Restricted area, authorized personnel only."

There's no one around and we run down the small corridor while Hank checks doors as we go, but they're all locked. He tries another door on the left. It's locked, and Hank, who is a pretty big guy, says, "Fuck that, I'm gonna bust it open." Before I can say anything, Hank, who's wearing big, heavy construction boots, kicks in the door right at the deadbolt. The door flies open and there's a loud *bang*, with wood splinters everywhere. We all rush in.

We're now in a large storage/utility room, filled with cleaning supplies, ladders, tools, and some old hockey equipment. The room stinks like mold and old sweat.

"So, now what?" I say.

Steve looks at me and says, "Yeah, really, what the fuck are we gonna do now? We can't go back out there, they're looking for us!"

"Thanks to you," I say. I think for about 30 seconds, while Hank and Steve, who are high, are starting to jump up and down and freak out a little. I tell Steve to switch jackets with me. He asks why and I tell him, "We need to split up. One of the cops already got a pretty good look at me, but if I have your coat, and he sees me again, he might not recognize me. They won't search me. Look, I have a baby face, I'm not high, and I don't smell like dope, unlike you guys. Plus, I don't think either of you can wipe those stupid permanent grins off your faces. Give me your coat and the dope. If they recognize and stop me, they'll probably only ask where you two are. I'll go out, and you guys take off the other way. If you get caught, they'll search you for sure, but you won't have anything on you."

"Why don't we leave the weed here and walk out the front way?" Steve says.

"Because we don't know what those guys told the cops. I just want to go home, and splitting up gives us the best chance of getting out of here without a problem. Plus, you guys still want that weed, don't you?"

I was naive, and a little too cocky in not thinking the cops would search me if I was stopped.

Hank tells Steve to give me his coat. Steve quickly switches jackets with me and I go back out to the main street-level open area, while Hank and Steve take off the other way, down the thin corridor, and out through a side exit of the Gardens.

It's busy but I don't see any cops, or the guys who were after us. I'm making my way through the crowd to the front doors, then out of nowhere, the cop who saw me at the top of the stairs steps out of the crowd, and he's almost right in front of me. I didn't even see him at first, and there is no way I can avoid him. He sees me, grabs my arm hard, and pulls me to the side. "I've seen you before, where are your buddies?" he says.

"What buddies? I'm alone," I say.

"Okay smart ass, open your coat."

"Why? I haven't done anything. You can't just search me for nothing. I just wanna go home."

"Open the coat, you little shit, or I'll rip it off you!"

I open the jacket, and the cop starts going through my outside pockets. He takes a pack of smokes and a lighter from the breast pocket of the jean jacket, and starts going through the cigarette pack, looking for joints, I guess. He finds nothing and tosses the smokes and lighter to the floor. The dope is in my left inside pocket. I had forgotten about Steve's little trick about putting the pot into my sock, but it's too late for that now.

As the cop is reaching into my inside pockets, I hear a whistle and the cop turns around while still holding on to me. I look up over the cop's shoulder and see the cop with the whistle motioning to the cop who's holding me. He lets go of me, looks me right in eye and says, "Get the fuck outta here, now!" I take his advice and walk to the front doors.

Relieved, and with my heart still pounding, I walk out of the Gardens as April Wine is finishing up their encore with "Roller."

High Roller Baby

Before I open the door to the street all I can hear is, "Bye bye, bye bye, bye bye. Bye bye, bye bye, bye bye." I sing along with them and walk out into the bright lights of Carlton Street. The clipped, close sounds and the far off low level hum of the big city, replaces the ear-splitting howling of the rock concert.

I meet up with Hank and Steve a block away on Yonge Street and we go into a dive bar, get a booth, and have a few beers. Tons of people are out on the street now, flowing out of the concert. We're sitting in a window booth and watching closely for the guys who were looking for us earlier, but we never see them.

Through all the commotion and how fast everything happened, I never got a chance to ask Steve how, or why, he stole the weed from those two guys. So I ask him.

Steve tells us he had gotten up to go to the washroom, and when he came out, two guys asked him if he wanted to buy some weed. He told us it was busy up on the landing as people were leaving the concert. He agreed to buy the weed and one of the guys took out a bag and gave Steve a price.

Just then, the guy holding the bag of weed got bumped from behind and dropped the baggie onto the floor, while at the same time more people were coming out of the concert and had gotten in between Steve and the guy selling the weed. So, Steve reached down, grabbed the baggie, and took off into the crowd. He thought he had lost the guys as he couldn't see them when he returned to his seat. The next thing he knew, I was telling him about two sketchy guys looking around at the top of our aisle, and he realized it was them.

We talk and laugh about what happened the next day at work. Steve apologizes to us for being stupid and almost getting us arrested or beat up. Hank thanks me for having the nerve to walk right up to the cops to create a diversion so they could get out of there. Then it's all forgotten and we go back to our normal routine of working, drinking beer, and trying to afford the payments and repairs on our cars so we can keep them running.

The Vodka
And Oranges Urban Myth

This little story happened at one of the many small print shops where I worked after leaving my first job. I believe it to be an urban myth, but I think the myth gave some guys the idea to try it themselves. I mean, why not, it's a good idea, and I actually witnessed it!

I had just left my first job in downtown Toronto and was now working at a small print shop off Yonge Street just north of St. Clair Avenue. I was 17 and it was the early spring of 1980. It was still a bit cold outside, and I was in between cars at the time. This meant I had to take the subway to work for the first few months I was there, but my commute was more than an hour each way and I couldn't handle that. My '73 Mercury Montego had about completely fallen apart, it had become undriveable, and I had to get rid of it. At the time, I wanted a more reliable car, which would cost more money than I had available, so I had to wait to save up some cash. Due to frustration with the commute, I ended up settling and buying a cheap car about six weeks into the job.

I worked at this print shop for a couple of years. Over that time, co-workers would come and go. We were all young and, at the time, moving from job to job was the norm. Although my first two jobs were stable and I stayed for a couple of years at both, I did change jobs frequently in my youth, but that didn't happen until after I left this print shop.

During my first few months at this job, a new bindery guy started working in the back of the shop. In most print shops there is a separate department called Bindery. The bindery employees didn't run any printing presses. They put together booklets, three-hole drilled finished print jobs, glued together the writing pads we had printed, and stapled items together. Sometimes they would have to handle shipping and receiving if the shop was small. It was a crappy job and I hated doing it, which happened whenever we were shorthanded, or had a big job on a short timeline where the printers had to help to get a particular order done. In this small shop, the bindery department took up almost half of the shop in the back. The shop was also open concept, so we could see the bindery area, which was about 50 feet away from the presses, and whoever was working there could see us.

The new bindery guy, Chip, was older than me but still young and in his early 20s. He didn't talk much, was nice and did his job well, but there was something about him the press operators couldn't get a handle on. After work on most Fridays, we would go out for beers at the bar next door. Chip never came with us, although we always invited him, and some afternoons he was very quiet.

One of the other pressmen, Hank, had some experience with the bindery machines and would go and help Chip sometimes. After helping Chip one afternoon, he came back to his press, which was right beside mine. When the presses were running, it was a bit loud, so you could talk without anyone hearing you if you were close to each other.

Hank told me he thought Chip was drunk. "Drunk?" I asked. "What makes you think that?"

"Well, he didn't understand right away what I was showing him as he usually does, and I'm almost positive he was slurring his words."

"Really," I said. "Well, that's interesting. That would explain him being quiet in the afternoons."

"It certainly would," Hank said.

"Did you smell alcohol on his breath?"

"Nope, nothing, and I was checking. I did see a few oranges under his worktable, though."

"So? I've seen him eat oranges too."

"No, there were like five oranges, and I see him eating them all the time. It just seems strange."

"Hmmm... I guess it is. I never noticed. What do you think is going on?"

"Well, I've got a pretty good idea."

"And that would be?"

"I'll show you tonight. We're both working late. After Chip leaves, we're going to go look for a few things."

"Like what?" I asked.

"Wait for tonight. If it's what I think it is, you'll laugh!"

"Oh, jeez. Okay."

Five o'clock comes around and everyone goes home except me, Hank, and David, the boss. David always stayed a little late to lock up, but tonight Hank and I planned to work until about eight o'clock. David came out of the front office at about 5:30 and asked if we were good for tonight and said he was going to lock up. We told him we were fine and said goodnight. He locked the doors, turned out the front office lights, and left through the back door.

Hank went to the back of the shop and watched for the boss to drive away. After that, he came back to his station, shut his press down, then told me to do the same.

"Okay, now we go look," Hank said. He waved for me to follow as he walked to the back of the shop.

"Oh shit," I said, "I forgot about the orange thing."

When we got to Chip's workspace, Hank said, "This is where we're going to look." At this point, the shop was completely silent, with only the sound being the heating fan running.

Hank reached down under Chip's work desk, pulled out about five or six oranges, and put them on top of the desk. "See, I knew it, this guy is a weirdo I tell ya."

"Well, maybe the guy likes oranges," I said.

The Vodka and Oranges Urban Myth

He reached down under the work desk again and pulled out a syringe. "Oh yeah? What about this?"

"Holy shit, the guy's a doper! I thought you said he was a drunk?"

"He's not a doper, you idiot, are you clueless or what? He's a drunk!"

"A drunk? Okay, I'm completely confused now."

"One last thing," Hank said. He then reached down under the desk again, brought up a mickey of vodka, and threw it onto the top of the work desk.

"This is what I was talking about this afternoon. I had an idea, but I had to make sure," Hank said to me.

"Okay, I have no idea what's going on here, please explain," I said.

"Oh, for cryin' out loud! He takes the vodka, fills the syringe, injects the vodka into an orange, then eats the orange. Bang! Instant screwdriver. Get it now, Todd?"

"Ohhh. Yup, I get it now, but jeez, I never thought about that. And you're right, that is funny! So, what now?"

"What do you mean, what now?"

"Well, what do we do now?"

"I'm going to talk to him tomorrow. I'm going to tell him I know what he's been doing and warn him that he needs to stop before David finds out. I'm also going to tell him he's lucky I found out before David did."

"Okay, but do you think he'll stop?"

"I have no idea, but I'm not going to snitch on him, that's for sure."

The next day was Friday, and I wasn't feeling well, so I left early, before Hank had a chance to talk to Chip.

When I came in on the following Monday, Chip wasn't there, which was strange as Chip had always been at work before we were. I was late, which wasn't unusual for me then, and Hank was late too. After I had settled in and I had my press up and running, Hank showed up, just after 9:30 a.m. and asked me where Chip was. I told him I didn't know, he hadn't shown up yet. I asked Hank if he had talked to Chip on Friday afternoon, and he said he had told him he knew what he was doing.

"Well, what did he say?" I asked.

"Nothing really. He said thanks and that he'd take care of it."

"You didn't press him on it? You didn't ask him what he was going to do?"

"Nope, he's an adult, he can do what he wants. I took it that he was going to stop drinking at work."

"Well, I guess we'll see."

And that was the end of that. Chip never came back to work. David asked us both if we knew what was going on with Chip and if we knew why he wasn't at work. We both told him we had no idea.

I never heard from Chip again, and neither did anyone else at the shop. I found out later from David that Chip never came back for his final paycheque. David tried to get ahold of him to pay him, but he never got anywhere with that. He couldn't find him anywhere.

I think about Chip sometimes and what became of him. But I never did find out. He just disappeared into the big city, like so many others during my teenage years.

Holy Shit. It's the Cops! Run!

After this story took place, my life started down a more "normal path," as they say. I started working a lot more, spending more time outside of Swansea, and spending time with Nancy. We began dating just short of a year before this event occurred. I still had some fun times and adventures, but those times didn't involve Swansea as much, and were uneventful, with a few exceptions, though we still lived in Swansea.

This story occurred in the summer of 1980, when I was 17. At the time, gas was about $1.20 a gallon. Our total take, if successful, would have been about 12 bucks, so it wasn't about the money, that's for sure. At the time, it was an adventure, to see if we could do it and get away with it, and it also had to do with beating our summer boredom.

I can't explain our thought processes at that time. We were young and I was never involved in anything even close to this before or after ever again – I can't explain that either. It could be I was growing up and becoming more mature. This incident did make me take a step back and think about what I had been doing. Maybe it was time for me to put away childhood things. I didn't want my bad behaviour to escalate. But it wasn't a fear of interaction with the police, I was never afraid of the police. I had always been ready for conflict, not that I wanted it or sought it out, but if it came up, I never shirked from it, and during my teenage years I had almost no respect for authority of any kind. I did what I wanted and was ready to face the consequences of my actions. I had no fear about that in any way.

The laws I broke as a kid all involved underage driving or drinking beer, but never at the same time. This was the one and only time I broke the law in this way. In other words, I was not then, nor have I ever been, a career criminal. Although I always did my best to make sure I didn't have to pay the price for what I did, I will say I was incredibly lucky. I used my wits and whatever resources were available to me to get out of some sticky situations, and that happened on occasion. I am much the same to this day when it comes to all that, but I don't break any laws. This story was a one-time deal at this level, but it wasn't the first time I had interactions with the police as a teenager.

It all started about seven o'clock on a Thursday evening. My two friends, Jim and Rob, had just arrived at the garage behind my house on Lavinia Avenue to sit around and have a few beers. We called it "Down the Back," as it was at the bottom of a whole lot of stairs that ran down the right side of the house, and two storeys lower than street level. You could access the garage from the laneway that ran out onto Durie Street. My '73 Toyota Corolla was parked in the driveway; I had just had it painted process blue, a deep pastel sky blue.

My parents never used the garage, so it was only me, my brothers, and our friends. In the late 70s, I turned the garage into a little rec room. I had put in a nice piece of indoor/outdoor carpet earlier that spring that covered about three-quarters of the floor. There was also an old fridge in the corner, and I got a big old couch from one of my mom's friends that I put against the north wall. The couch was from the 60s. It was huge, about nine feet long, and super ugly, but it was also in great condition and very comfortable. I had a cassette player and a wood-burning furnace for the winter that my older brother built out of an old, rusted, 45 gallon drum. It wasn't the nicest, but it was my own little space. In 1970s Swansea, freedom and contentment from the outside world was easy to acquire, and I took advantage of that freedom whenever I could.

Holy Shit. It's the Cops! Run!

In the summer, I would spend weekend afternoons – or weekdays when I didn't feel like going to work – lying on the couch reading or listening to music all by myself. I read a lot of literature in my teenage years, including *Crime and Punishment, The Great Gatsby, Flowers for Algernon*, some Steinbeck, a book by Émile Zola, and also a lot of science fiction. I enjoyed reading. None of my friends read like I did, and I never told anyone I was reading that stuff, though I don't know why. It was so quiet Down the Back at times; I would fall asleep while reading, the only sound being the birds chirping in the trees. *The Grapes of Wrath* was one of the books I read in a few days that summer. I cried at the end of it, all alone, and then fell asleep for an hour.

Rob had brought up the idea of siphoning gas first, by asking if I could get a couple of five-gallon metal drums from work. At the time, I worked at a small print shop running a printing press, and we used some pretty strong solvents to wash the presses. The solvents came in those drums. We threw out the empty ones anyway so I said I could get a few and bring them home for the weekend. We had a few more beers while listening to Supertramp on the cassette player. I was tired and had a big day at work coming up on Friday, so they eventually left.

Saturday rolls around. I work until noon and get home around 1 p.m. I'm not tired, so I clean out the three feet of fast-food garbage from the back of the car. I put one of the five-gallon drums I took from work in the trunk and one in the back seat, and then I read *This Perfect Day* by Ira Levin for a while on the couch in the garage before falling asleep. I wake up about an hour later. It was nice how quiet it could be at times Down the Back.

Jim and Rob show up a few hours later and Rob brings a four-foot piece of green garden hose to use as a siphon. We discuss where we're going to go, I don't want to start siphoning gas right out on the street. Jim suggests we try the condos down in South Swansea and we all agree. We wait for it to get a little darker, and then we all get in the car. We go down to the condos, but the parking lots are too open and lit up, so that's out. I say to try behind the apartment buildings on Windermere Avenue. We drive over and it's perfect – dark, out of the way, and quiet. We later find out it was too quiet.

We find a car and Jim starts the first setup. The siphon starts to work right away, and the first drum fills up fast. Jim stops the siphon and puts the drum in the trunk of the car. We see another car close to a fence, where it's a little darker. Rob and I flip a coin to see who will start the siphon for the second drum and I lose. I set it all up and try to get it going, but it's not working well. I have to stop, too much gas is getting into my mouth, and I start to throw up a little. When I finish throwing up from the gas, I try again, but I still can't get the gas to flow into the second drum without it stopping.

Suddenly, Jim says in a loud whisper, "Holy shit. It's the cops! Run!" I guess we weren't as quiet as we thought. I get up and look to my right. Behind the fence between the apartment building on Coe Hill Drive and the parking lot we are in, about ten feet from me, I can see the cop. I look him straight in the eye; neither of us can completely see each other's faces. It's dark, and the trees on his side close to the fence are obscuring our views. He doesn't say anything, which I find strange, but I can see as he moves closer, he has an "I gotcha!" look on his face.

Jim and Rob take off west towards Windermere, while I run south about 20 feet down the line of the fence, then turn and continue east along the fence through the laneway that separates the last apartment building on Coe Hill from Swansea Mews, a large public housing complex at the south end of Swansea. The cop is keeping good pace with me on the other side of the fence. About halfway down the laneway, there is a small break in the trees and someone yells out from their window, "Hey, there he is!"

As the cop shadows me along the fence line, I know something he doesn't – he has no way out, while I am less than 100 feet from the open street. I reach the street as the laneway ends after what feels like forever but is actually less than half a minute. The cop is out of the chase as the fence runs out, and he is now blocked from me by the connecting fence that runs north and south. I know that I've won, so I stop. For just a second, I turn, and once again look at him through the fence and trees.

He is now partially illuminated from a streetlight across the street and a little north of us, but I am still mostly in shadow, as the streetlight at the end of the laneway where I am standing is out, and there is no moon.

I remember he looked young and not much older than me. The smirk he had worn was replaced with a look of incredulity. He looked around for an out but found himself surrounded by fencing. He knew right there I had him, and he threw his hands up in the air. It was then I turned around and walked south down Coe Hill and into the darkness of the quiet evening.

I walk less than 20 feet when I hear the klaxon horn of the police car followed by two quick *whoop whoop* sounds of the siren behind me. I turn around and see the cop car about 50 feet from me and the headlights are turned off. I hear the engine rev as I take off down the driveway of the first house on the west side of the street, south of the apartment building on Coe Hill. I run down the driveway and into the back yard, where I stop and look around. *How can I get out?* I think to myself.

I hear the cop car door slam, and I know he is coming for me; I have no time to think. To the right of me is a long line of thick bushes, so I run over and lie down behind the thickest bushes that are against the fence separating the back yard from the small footpath leading into Swansea Mews. The footpath runs parallel to the fence I have just been chased along by the young cop. I am right against the back of the house, my heart pounding out of my chest. I see a flashlight coming down the driveway as the cop enters the back yard. He stops to shine his light around the back yard, and then in complete silence, he starts to walk around. He makes it to the end of the back yard and starts to come back down the fence line, using his light to see if I am there. I know right then he will see me when he reaches the end of the fence where I'm hiding.

As his light gets closer, I think of running out and down the driveway. I have only seconds to think, but I don't know if there is another cop in the car on the street at the end of the driveway waiting for me or not, so I stay where I am.

He's right on top of me now with his flashlight shining in my face, but he makes no move towards me. *Can he not see me? Unbelievable! But if he can't see me, why isn't he leaving?* All I can do is not move nor breathe. After bending, looking closer, and seeing nothing, he gets up and walks away, down the driveway.

I listen for the cop car to drive away for what seems like a long time, but I hear nothing. Maybe I didn't hear the car door close, so I get up and walk across the grass to the driveway. Just then, I see a flashlight coming down the next driveway to the south. I don't have time to go back to my hiding place without him seeing me, so I stand flat against the side of the house. Even if he looks over again, he won't see me. I stay still and quiet with sweat dripping down my forehead into my eyes, and wait for the cop to look around the second back yard, but he finds nothing and leaves. I hear the car door close, followed by the cop car driving away. I slowly walk down the driveway, making sure to stick close to the house.

When I reach the street, I crouch down and then pop up cautiously, looking for anyone, but the street is empty, dark, and quiet.

I don't want to walk north since the cop may still be looking for me, but I do anyway. It's the shortest path home if I can't get to my car. I get to the lane that the cop chased me down. *Maybe I can make it back to my car,* I think. I can see the lights of multiple cop cars in the parking lot and they have my car. "Awww shit!" I say to myself. It's a big risk to go north now, so I turn around and walk south down Coe Hill to Ellis Gardens, then east over to Ellis Avenue. I start the long walk north up Ellis, sticking close to the sides of the street. I'm very nervous, and with every car that comes up or down the street, I run into any hiding spot I can find, but I don't come across any cops.

Holy Shit. It's the Cops! Run!

I know there are two sets of stairs on Ellis Avenue that can take me into Catfish Pond marsh, and one set of stairs farther up the street that can take me into Rennie Park. I decide I want to get home as fast as I can, so taking a chance, I go for the stairs near the top of the street. I don't see any more cars coming up the street, and I soon make it to the stairs. I quickly run down them and I'm in the park behind the rink and tennis courts. The park is dark and quiet; no one is around. I run through the park diagonally, south to north, to the corner bench at Morningside Avenue and Beresford Avenue, up Morningside, then north on Durie Street to the lane that takes me to the back of my house. I'm tired, sweating, and stressed by the time I try the door after running up the stairs to the front of my house, but it's locked.

My mom works nights as a nurse sometimes, and my dad moonlights a second job. I search for my house keys but realize I left them on the keychain with my car keys, which I left in the ignition of my car in case we had to get out of there fast.

My brother Kim doesn't live at the house anymore and my brother Mike lives with his wife in the basement apartment of the house. I don't know if he is home and I want to get off the street. I'm looking around thinking the cops could show up at any second, and I'll be caught. I knock on the door hoping my other brother Glenn is awake, but there is no answer. *Shit, what am I going to do?* I think to myself. Then, Glenn suddenly opens the door and I rush in. I go upstairs to my bedroom, throw myself onto my bed, and quickly fall asleep. I'm home free – or so I think.

I'm sleeping for about half an hour when there's a knock on my bedroom door and I figure it's Glenn wanting something. I yell through the door for Glenn to go away, and that I'm sleeping. The door opens anyway, and I see the beams from two flashlights bouncing around the room. I look up to see the silhouettes of two giant cops in my room calling my name. They point their lights at the bed and I immediately get up and sit on the edge of it.

The Life of a 1970s Teenager

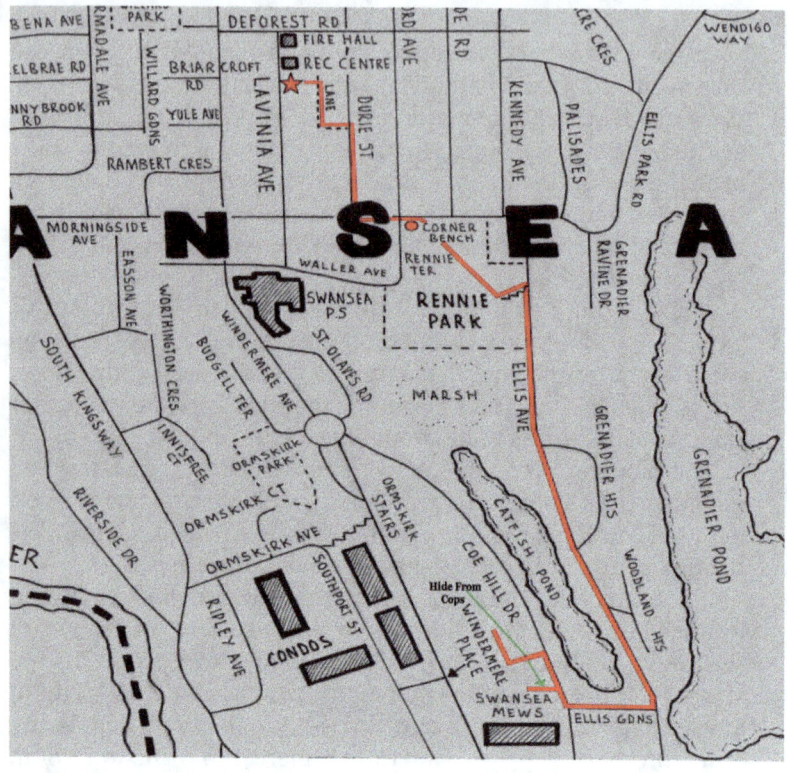

Map of my escape route from the cops. From behind 75 Windermere Ave, to my house, the Red Star.

"Are you Todd Bueler?" one of them asks, shining his light in my face.

"Can ya get the light out of my face, please?" I say, and he moves the light to the side. For a second, I think I will tell them no, I'm his brother Mike, and I don't know where Todd is, but I change my mind and say yes, I'm Todd.

I ask them what the hell they're doing in my house, and how did they get in?!

One cop says the gentleman downstairs let them in.

Holy Shit. It's the Cops! Run!

I say, "That's my brother Glenn, he's mentally handicapped, and he doesn't know that he shouldn't have let you in."

The cop says, "Sorry, but since we're here, could you come downstairs? We need to talk to you about something."

"About what?" I ask snarkily.

"We have your car."

"You have my car? Why would you have my car?"

"It would be best if we went downstairs to talk, sir."

They are polite, I'll give them that.

We go downstairs and I sit on the couch with the two cops standing in front of me. Glenn is there and I tell him I need to speak to these policemen, it's his bedtime, and he should go upstairs. Glenn says okay and goes up to bed. Right off the bat the good cop, bad cop thing starts. They tell me not only do they have my car, but where, how, and why they have it. They ask me if I have any idea how that all happened. I tell them I have no idea.

The older cop, who is playing bad cop, says he thinks it was me who was chased, and that I know very well what happened because I was there. And, unless I can come up with a good explanation, they are going to arrest me right there.

Good cop, the younger cop, says, "Hold on. Todd, were you there?"

"No."

"How did your car get there?"

"All I know is the last time I saw my car was earlier tonight down the back of my house in the driveway."

"Do you have the keys?"

"I must've left them in the ignition and forgot to bring them in."

Bad cop says, "The whole damn house stinks of gas!" He's right, it does stink.

"I was working on the carburetor of the car and got some gas on me."

"You expect us to believe that?"

"That's what happened," I say.

"So, you're reporting the car stolen?"

193

"No. All I'm saying is the last time I saw my car was down the back earlier tonight. Now you say you have it. I don't know how you got it, or how it got to be where you said it was. When can I get it back?"

Good cop says, "Todd, let's go out front so we can talk." I say okay, and we go outside, leaving bad cop inside.

My house is about eight feet below street level, so there are about five or six steps from the front door going up to the sidewalk. It's one of those rare nights where it's getting hotter as the night goes on. As we walk outside, the heat and humidity hits us like a brick wall. Good cop goes out first and walks up a few steps before he stops. I'm now looking up at him.

He's speaking nicely, quietly, and calmly. He tells me they know what happened and there is another cop who can identify me as being there. I tell him I doubt that as I have been here all night.

"Look, Todd, it's not a big deal. Just tell us what happened so we don't have to keep looking for someone else. A lot of young people make mistakes, and we understand that. This is not a serious thing. We're not going to do anything to you, we're not going to arrest you. We just need the truth."

Wow, this guy is good, but I don't believe him. If I admit it was me, they are going to arrest me for sure. If I learned one thing about dealing with cops at the time, when they tell you something, like when bad cop said he was going to arrest me, believe them! I know about the whole good cop, bad cop thing, and I tell him I understand, but I wasn't there. Bad cop comes out of the house, and just then my brother, who lives in the apartment downstairs, appears at the top of the side stairs. He must have heard all the walking around in the living room and came up to see what was going on, since it's late. Good thing I didn't say I was Mike before!

Mike looks at me, then the cops, and then asks what's going on. Bad cop asks him who he is, and what he's doing there. Mike tells him who he is and that he lives downstairs. Again, he asks what's going on. Bad cop starts to explain why they are there, and that I'm in trouble.

As bad cop is explaining the whole situation to my brother and what I told him happened, another cop car pulls up in front of the house. I look up and I'm thinking to myself, *Who am I, Al Capone? Was it the Mayor's gas I stole?*

The newly arrived officer gets out of his car and walks to the top of the stairs. I look at him, and wouldn't ya know it, it's the same cop who chased me down the fence line! *Crap, is this ever going to end?*

The officers all acknowledge each other with nods, and bad cop continues talking. Then chase cop looks at me, then over at my brother, then back at me for a long time, squinting his eyes a little. I look away, but I don't put my head down, and bad cop is still telling the story to my brother. I look back up at chase cop, and he's still looking at me. *This is it; I'm busted,* I think. But he makes no move towards me and says nothing. Ha! Now I know.

He doesn't recognize me. I can't believe it, but I keep my composure, and I give no quarter. I was pretty sure he didn't get a good look at me before, but I wasn't positive until now. Both me and chase cop look back at bad cop as he's finishing up the story.

Bad cop finishes and is waiting for my brother's reply.

Mike says, "Is that it?" My brother didn't say it, but I knew he was thinking, *That's all you got, cop?*

"That's it," says bad cop. My brother looks over at me and he almost smiles. If this was a movie, he'd be looking right into the camera with a surprised look of, "Can you believe this?" Of course, he thought it was a bunch of crap, as did both cops, but a damn good story just the same.

My brother then turns to the cop and says, "Well, if that's what he told you, then that's what happened."

Bad cop isn't happy with that and shakes his head. I don't know what he thought my brother would say. Did he think he would say I was a liar? I wasn't using him as an alibi, so I wasn't sure what bad cop was trying to get out of this.

"Well, is that it?" I ask. "Anything else?"
"Yes, that's all," good cop says, "and no, there's nothing else."
"When can I get my car back?"
"Come to the station tomorrow afternoon and you can get a release form."
"Great, thanks for all your help."
"Okay, have a good night."

They walk up the stairs in their big black boots. As good cop gets to the top stair, he turns around and says, "You know, Todd, you're over 16 now. In the eyes of the law, you're an adult. Your time as a kid has ended, things have changed. You need to be careful." With that statement right there, I knew I was right not telling good cop I was there when he told me it wasn't a big deal earlier. Then they get into their yellow cop cars and drive away. My brother turns to go back to his apartment and says, "I'm not taking you to get your car tomorrow. You're very lucky."

"I know. See ya."

The next day I get another buddy of mine to drive me up to the old 11 Division police station on Mavety Street. We walk into the station, and I tell the desk sergeant I need a release form for my car. I tell him my name, and he says to hold on. He goes into the back, then returns a few minutes later and tells me I need to see an officer who wants to talk to me before he releases the car. I wait while he looks down at some papers and tells me the officer who wants to see me isn't on shift until the evening. I tell him I need my car, and could he please release the car and I'll come to see the officer tonight. He makes a face, thinks for a bit, and then says okay. We wait for a little longer as he fills out the release form and gives it to me. I know right then nothing will come of the night before, else he wouldn't have released the car to me.

Now that I have the release form, we drive up to the impound lot near the Stockyards a few blocks north.

I show the release form to the lot manager, he gives me the keys, and shows us to my car.

The car is unlocked and when I open the door, I see that all the papers that were in the glove compartment are scattered all over the front seat and floor, but the glove compartment is closed.

As I open the glove compartment and start cleaning up the mess, a very personal letter I had written a few weeks before falls from the top where it was stuck onto the glove compartment door latch. The letter unfolds as it falls but is still stuck on the door latch so you can read it hanging there. I look at the letter and laugh. Those cops sure were pissed at me. I take the letter down, clean up the rest of the papers, and drive home. I never went back to the police station that night, or any night, and the cops never contacted me again about the previous evening.

Oh, and what happened to Jim and Rob that night? Well, nothing. They took off west towards Windermere, and I ran east. While I was being chased by the cop down the fence line, they walked home, uneventfully.

Postscript

Dreaming Again

I had been writing a lot during the fall of 2022. I was writing a few stories at the same time, going back and forth between them for about a week straight with no break. I was writing every day, which is unusual for me.

I don't write every day as it takes a lot out of me, or sometimes I just don't feel like it. My normal writing schedule is in short bursts, writing 500, 1,000, or 2,000 words in a day or two, then no writing for a few days or sometimes weeks.

During the time when I was writing every day, I had been experiencing some very vivid dreams at night. Some were nice, good memories; others were downright frightening. I'm pretty sure it was from me constantly thinking about the past. This didn't bother me, though, and some of the dreams were very realistic, but I think that's normal.

Here's a short dream I had near the end of that every day writing stint. I almost never remember those dreams in any detail, but this one was different for some reason. The dream was of me running from the cops in the previous story. This was a strange time to dream about the story, as it was complete – it had all been edited and finalized months earlier. After I woke up, the dream was so clear in my mind; I wrote it down right away. This incident, unlike the story, didn't even happen in real life, only in my dream.

I make it to the picnic/Coochie Dome in Rennie Park and quickly run to the green park bench that is on the far side. I crawl under the bench to hide from the flashing red and blue lights that are all around me now. It's dark, hot, and humid. My long curly hair is dripping with sweat, my thin t-shirt is soaked, and my mouth is dry; I'm out of breath. All I can hear is the wind whipping through the trees on the hill that is right beside the dome and the crackling of the police car radio that is parked at the top of the hill on Rennie Terrace. The radio is barking out call signals and where my last known location was.

Should I bolt through the park and try to make it to the street, or sit and wait to see if the cops come into the park to look for me? I decide I can't stay where I am.

I run north into the park from under the bench and stick close to the bottom edge of the small grass hill that runs the length of the park, south to north on the west side, below the street level of Rennie Terrace. I make it to the end of the park and onto the street. When I look back, the cops are just coming down the hill and into the dome on foot. They don't see me, and I run up Morningside Avenue. I reach the south end of Durie Street and, turning right, I head north and run down the hill to the lane. I walk into the lane that takes me to the back yard of my house; there's not a cop in sight. I walk a few feet into my back yard and stop to catch my breath in the quiet, dark of the night.

Holy Shit. It's the Cops! Run!

It's twilight now, and I find myself standing in front of my house at 85 Lavinia, looking east as the sun peeks above the horizon, I close my eyes and tilt my head upwards. I wait in the quiet hush of the dew-soaked morning as the warmth of the sunrise envelops me. I hear a torrent of fast-moving water below me and I open my eyes. There are no houses now, only trees as I look down into the deep green of the Swansea valley. The sun is sparkling on the surface of the fast flowing river now and I squint.

I see the power of the never-ending, crystal-clear water as it cuts southeast to Durie, then dips farther past Durie into Beresford, evening out and turning south at Morningside through Rennie Park, before dipping again and rushing the 200 yards into Catfish Pond. I once read that the old river widened out at Deforest as it continued its unstoppable path coming from the north. But that was hundreds, maybe even thousands of years ago. How can it possibly be here now? How can an ancient river run through my back yard? It's 1980! Am I dreaming again? I don't know, it's all so real.

I feel cold, and I jolt upright in my bed, my heart beating fast. I'm breathing hard, and I'm confused. I have never been so frightened in my life. I look around and see the bright moonlight coming through the window and realize I am safely at home, in my bed. I guess writing this book has affected me more than I thought.

The Rolling Stones

In the summer of 1981, I was 18. Like most teenagers of the time, music was a big part of our lives, and we went to a lot of rock concerts. We found out the Rolling Stones were coming to Rich Stadium, now known as Highmark Stadium, close to Buffalo. The trip from Swansea to Buffalo is about two hours long, and Orchard Park, where the stadium is located, is about 20 minutes farther. Nancy, who was my girlfriend at the time, my buddy Daniel and I, found a guy in the newspaper who was scalping tickets for the concert. We met him at Jane and Bloor streets, and he wanted $100 for each ticket. At the time, the average box office price per ticket was $16 each, so we told him to... well... you know. We ended up paying $60 each for the three tickets, which was a lot of money back then.

On September 27th, we drove to the border in my old '73 Toyota Corolla. In those days, a passport was not required to enter the USA. When we got to the border, the Customs and Border Patrol (CBP) officer asked us for our IDs. Daniel, who had long hair down to his ass, told the CBP officer he forgot his ID. I looked at Daniel for a long time in disbelief. He told us to pull over for inspection, so we did. Four CBP officers proceeded to totally rip apart my whole car as they searched it and, of course, didn't find anything. As they walked away, one of the officers said, "Ya know, just because you're going to the Stones concert, doesn't mean we have to let you in." We just stood there, and again I'm just staring at Daniel. Then the officer says, "Just go!"

The Rolling Stones

We made it to the show, and it was both good and bad. When Journey performed, they got booed off the stage. George Thorogood's performance was great. It rained a little during the concert and the saxophone player for Thorogood wiped out and fell flat on his ass.

When the Stones came out to perform, Keith Richards must have been high or drunk or both, he kept screwing up badly and Mick Jagger's voice was awful. At the beginning of one of the songs, Keith kept playing the same opening chords over and over again about 15 times, like he had forgotten the next part. It was embarrassing.

In summary, the Stones' performance was terrible, Journey got booed off the stage, and Thorogood was amazing. I still have the ticket stubs from this concert.

The Postman
Gets Knocked Down Twice

In late November of 1987, I was 25 and had been married only a few months earlier at Morningside-High Park Presbyterian Church in Toronto. My new wife Nancy and I had recently moved into the basement apartment of my family home on Lavinia Avenue, and I had started a new job at the post office as a letter carrier. They called them postmen back then. I lasted three days.

In the 80s, the post office would give you a route close to home; I was stationed at the old post office on the south side of Bloor Street, between Willard Avenue and Armadale Avenue.

The job began with a preliminary mail sort at one of the big depots in the city. Then the pre-sorted items were brought to your local postal station early in the morning. Letter carriers started at 6:30 a.m. at the station, beginning their final sort for the day's deliveries. After completing the sort for your route, you were ready to go out. The final sort would take about three hours.

After your sort, you filled up your mailbag for the first round of deliveries. For the rest of the route, you gave filled mailbags, sorted for each load along the way, to a driver. The driver would go around your route and drop off your bags at those green metal boxes you used to see on the street – I think they were called relay boxes – while you were delivering elsewhere. Letter carriers had a key for the relay boxes along their route, and as you ran out of mail, you would pick up your next batch and continue delivering. I never worked in the summer, but the guys told me the drivers would also leave cold bottles of water or cans of beer in the boxes for you.

My route was nice enough, though a little broken up. I started in the Humber Valley, off Jane Street north of Baby Point Road. When I finished delivering in the Valley, I would drive south and work my way back towards the station, delivering through the streets east of Jane, south of Colbeck Street. You didn't have to go back to the station if you didn't want to after your route was finished; you could just go home. So the faster you did your route, the fewer hours you worked, but you were paid for the full day. I had learned my route well, and by the second day I had already gone home an hour early.

I still hadn't received my postman uniform by the third day, and I knew it would be cold, so I wore my heavy Carhartt canvas coat to keep warm. This seemingly innocent decision would prove to save my life that day, as did my thick canvas mailbag.

It was pitch black outside that morning, but I could see my breath under the big bright streetlights as I sat alone in my car in front of my house, warming it up to drive the few short blocks to the sorting centre. Then, it started to snow. It fell lightly at first, then got heavy – big, thick flakes slowly, silently floating to the ground. Within minutes the ground was covered, a brilliant white against the morning's quiet, cold darkness. It made for a beautiful scene looking out my windshield down Lavinia towards Deforest Road.

I got to the station and went to my little route-sorting work area. All the guys were there, laughing, doing their sorts, and complaining about the cold and snow. I will admit most of them were real jerks. The only guys I liked and got along with were the drivers. The other postmen were pretentious and rude. They would make little passive aggressive comments to me, and to the other guys about me, acting like I couldn't hear them, when obviously I could, though none of that bothered me. So I ignored them, and I think it pissed them off.

I enjoyed doing my sort, going out on my route, and the customers I met were also very nice. I finished my sort, grabbed my mailbag, and drove up to the valley to start my route, beginning on a cul-de-sac street called Juliana Court at the valley's north end.

It was cold and still snowing, with almost no wind. My mailbag was full and heavy, and I delivered to the first three houses, opening and closing the mailbox lids as I went. It was quiet on the street, and the metal lids echoed around the cul-de-sac as I opened and closed them. I walked up the driveway of the fourth house, delivered their mail, and closed the lid. I walked down the three stairs and turned to walk back down the driveway.

As I stepped onto the driveway and turned towards the street, out of nowhere and without a sound, something hit me from behind and knocked me to the ground. I turned my head and saw a huge German Shepherd dog jumping back over the house's fence, disappearing behind the five feet of solid wood. A little shaken, I picked myself up and continued walking down the driveway, while looking around as I took in hurried breaths. Seconds later, the dog jumped back over the fence, and this time, I heard him.

I turned around just as he lunged, putting my right arm up to block him. Sinking his teeth into my wrist, the dog had no trouble knocking me to the ground for a second time. Now on top of me, the dog began violently shaking his head with my wrist in his mouth. I started to hit him in the head with my left hand, but it was no use. Soon he was dragging me down the driveway; there was incredible pain in my wrist and blood pouring out onto the ground and soaking my coat sleeve.

When we reached the street, he let go of my wrist and started to go for my neck. Screaming, I pulled my mailbag up closer to my neck, gripping it as hard as I could as the dog bit into the bag, tearing it as he shook his head back and forth. I could feel his hot breath on my face and saw mail falling onto the ground as the bag's heavy canvas began to give way. I punched him three or four more times as hard as I could, desperate to escape as more blood spurted out of my wrist. Then, as quickly as the attack started, it ended. I watched as he leapt off me, ran up the driveway, and jumped over the fence once more.

In shock, I lay in the street, with blood and mail all over the road. It was completely silent and I looked up to the sky as the snow slowly fell, and passed out.

When I awoke, there was a middle-aged woman in a housecoat and boots standing over me, asking if I was alright. I told her, "No, I don't think so, and could you please help me?" She helped me up and walked me to her house a few steps away.

I sat in her kitchen as she told me about the screams she had heard moments earlier. She said by the time she came out, the dog was running away. She gave me a cup of hot coffee as I sat bleeding on her kitchen table, going in and out of consciousness. I didn't know where I was or what was happening. I must have passed out a few times; I remember her asking my name but only seeing darkness when I looked up to answer her. At least I thought I was looking up.

Soon I heard a loud knock at the front door, then some talking. I lifted my head from the table, or someone did. A woman and a man in blue uniforms were standing in front of the table.

"Todd? Todd? Can you hear me?" the woman asked.

"Yes, I can hear you," I replied.

It was the paramedics she had called. "C'mon, Todd, we're going to take you to the hospital and fix you up." She reached down and pulled on my underarm. "Can you walk?" she asked.

"Yes, I think so," I said.

"Okay, let's go."

"Where are we going?"

"We're going to the hospital."

"Oh, okay. But we better not go out that way, there's a dog attacking people out there."

"It's okay, the dog is gone now."

"Are you sure? I don't want to go out. I saw a big dog attack a postman earlier. There was blood all over the road. I hope he's okay."

"He's okay, Todd, and the dog is gone. Let's go now."
"Okay."

Outside, there was bright red blood staining the snow and blood-covered mail scattered all over the road. Two police cars sat in the middle of the street, and everything turned to slow motion. Walking out of the house, I looked side to side, and a police officer was looking at me as I stepped up into the ambulance parked at the end of the driveway.

It took seven stitches to close the huge hole in my wrist, and I still have the scar. The police interviewing me in the hospital told me animal control had seized the dog. After I answered their questions, they told me they were pretty sure the dog had heard the mailbox lids opening and shutting louder and louder as I got closer to his house. The officer said the dog was probably lying in wait for me, and he broke off the attack not because I was hitting him, but because I was off his property. I never returned to the post office after that day.

Return to School

By the time I was 24, I was married, and my wife and I had been living on our own since we were 21. As mentioned in a previous story, I left school at age 15 with a Grade 8 education. During that time, I tried many different jobs, but found myself continually returning to running a printing press to make money, a job I grew to hate more and more with each passing day.

I had had it with the crappy jobs that I could get with my limited education; I hated them all. I thought I would try to become a police officer, but I needed a high school diploma to do that, so I convinced the Toronto School Board to let me take six Grade 13 courses to get my diploma. They didn't want to let me do that as they didn't think I would be successful as I had no real academic background. It was difficult to convince them, but in the end they agreed.

I worked full and part-time jobs for 15 months while attending day and night classes to get those credits. It was hard to be an adult student in classes filled with 18-year-old kids, and I had to go to four different high schools throughout the city to take the courses I needed. This was the only way I could get into classes that fit into my schedule. I did not take any math classes, I only had a Grade 8 math level and knew there was no way I could get through the advanced Grade 13 math. Plus I didn't need it to get the diploma. This would be an issue for me later.

Once I had completed the classes, I received my Ontario Secondary School Honours Diploma. My marks were decent: two As, three Bs, and one C. With the diploma, I qualified for and applied to become a police officer in Toronto. Before I applied, I had very bad eyesight, 20/400 in both eyes, so I was legally blind. I had been wearing glasses since I was in my early teens, and although my eyesight was bad, wearing glasses did correct my vision. Technology at that time had advanced so much that you didn't have to wear the thick lenses normally associated with poor eyesight. Having uncorrected eyesight to the degree I had, though, disqualified me from becoming a police officer.

I had heard about a new surgical procedure that could correct your eyesight down to a possible 20/20 level, even with my bad numbers. It wasn't totally new, but it had become widely available, and it was expensive. The procedure was called Radial Keratotomy (RK). RK preceded the now popular laser eye surgery, LASIK, and the cost was $2,500 total for both eyes. That was a lot of money at the time, but I could make payments.

With RK, the ophthalmologist uses a sapphire scalpel and cuts your cornea in five or more places, in a radial fashion, meaning from the pupil out to the edge of the iris. This flattens the cornea, focusing the light to hit the retina in the right place. It was a difficult decision to have the surgery as there were risks involved. In the end, I had the surgery over a two-month period. Once the first eye was completed, the other was done six weeks later. My surgery was successful, and it gave me an uncorrected 20/20 in one eye and 20/40 in the other.

These new vision numbers were enough to pass the police department eye test. I trained hard for the physical test and knew I wouldn't have a problem with the written and psychological tests. I passed all three tests with ease, but I failed at the interview stage. They don't tell you why you failed, just that you didn't make it. I continued working in low-level, low-paying jobs for a few years after that, and I was miserable.

Let me back up a little bit. I had an old teacher for Grade 13 Canadian History while I pursued my diploma. I failed miserably on the first test I took in that class. I said to myself, *How can that be? Is my life going to be relegated to this depressing existence I've been living forever?* I was so confused.

One day, I noticed my teacher was looking at my wedding ring; I normally sat near the front of the class. She asked me to stay after class that day, and I did as she requested. She mentioned my wedding ring and asked if I was married. I told her I had gotten married that past summer. She then asked me what I was doing in high school at my age. I told her most of the details about leaving school early in life, having only a Grade 8 education, and about wanting to become a police officer. She told me she could help me if I wanted her to, and I told her I would very much appreciate that. I would stay after class a few times a week and she would personally tutor me; once we started, she taught me how to highlight relevant information in a textbook. She also taught me how to ignore all the unnecessary information in a paragraph, and how to pull out what was pertinent. These small but important skills changed my life. She also taught me the three main points on how to write a test or exam and be successful every time:

- Read the question
- Understand the question
- Answer the question

These three points may seem simple after reading them, but being aware of them and applying them helped me immensely.

I was a fast learner and caught on right away. On the very next test, I scored a 90. I was so happy, and I thanked her greatly for helping me.

At the end of the course, she again asked me to stay after class. She told me something that day that once again would change my life forever, but those changes would not take effect until five years later.

She told me I was too smart to continue with the career path I wanted without a post-secondary education. She told me I needed to find a way to go to university. She also said, and this may sound cliché, that I was destined for better things in my life, and going to university would give me more choices no matter what I did in the future. I thanked her and went home. I should have listened to her then. Not that I didn't think she was right, but I couldn't afford to go to university or college at that time, nor could I fit it into my busy schedule.

Again, I was making the same mistake I had in the past, not finding a way to further my education. Of course, this begs the question – why was I so reluctant to go to school? Why didn't I just do it? Was I only making excuses, or was it my propensity to not conform? And what about me wanting to become a police officer? Was that not about conformity? Quite a dichotomy, or was it? No, at the time I was just looking for a career. It didn't matter what it was, as I wasn't directly thinking about things in that way then. I knew I couldn't work in a factory doing what for me was boring work. I hated physical labour that brought with it no intellectual stimulation.

Could it be it was my constant refusal to conform to societal norms, subconsciously, that prevented me from re-applying to the police force? Did I think in the end my becoming a police officer went against my personal non-respect of authority? Evaluating the past is a tricky thing, and I have asked these questions of myself many, many times. I think the answer to some of these questions is yes. At the same time, to be truthful, not all my decisions to not return to school earlier were in my power. There are times when things can't be done or it's a better decision to leave them for later. At times, we all try to justify our own actions, whether they are right or wrong. I think in the end, my reasons for not returning to school are a combination of all of the above. We all live within the confines of our own contradictions in life. For me, it's a matter of being able to see those contradictions when they are happening in real time and being able to act on that awareness when needed. Who can ever see the correct path to take when presented with a fork in the road without foreknowledge of what lies ahead? It is almost an impossibility for me, and for most others, I'm guessing. One thing I am sure of though is this: I don't always know what the right thing to do is, but I always know what the wrong thing to do is. This was some-

Return to School

thing I learned about myself as I became an adult – and it deals mostly with ethical decisions, but not always.

I continued with my mundane life for the next three years. I was so depressed about what was happening to me. I hated going to work, and with a few exceptions, I hated the jobs I was working. I had ruled out trying to become a police officer and I can't remember why. I could have reapplied, but I think after my first failure I had lost interest for the profession. The year I turned 28, I had had enough, again, and I decided I couldn't keep working dead-end jobs anymore.

Nancy and I had a long talk one day in the spring of 1990. I told her I needed to do something to change the path I was on. As my wife, she supported me and agreed, so I applied to Seneca College for the three-year Computer Science program. I had never touched a computer in my life, but I was intrigued by the idea. There was only one problem; to get into college, I needed to have Grade 12 math. I only had Grade 8 math and I had not taken any math classes since. I was tenacious back then, and I enrolled in a summer school Grade 12 math class right before the fall semester at Seneca began. It was killer. I had no stepping stones from any high school math classes to help me to get through the Grade 12 course. But I jumped right in, hopping from the Grade 8 math I had taken 15 years before, to Grade 12 math. In the end, I received help from some of my friends from Swansea who did finish high school. I was able to get a grade of 67, which was enough to pass the course and get the credit so I would be accepted at Seneca that fall.

I don't think I would have gone on to college if it wasn't for my Grade 13 history teacher showing me how to highlight text and telling me she thought I should go to university. I'll never forget that teacher, Edith Cornett, and how she believed in me and those conversations we had together all those years ago. She changed my life.

Edith spent most of her career as a history teacher and department head at Mimico High School. She retired in 1988, one year after she taught me. Miss Cornett would have been 60 years old when she taught me history at Mimico High School in 1987. For a young man of 25, that was old. She was very intelligent. She knew how to talk to me and motivate me in a way that would reach me. I was very lucky to have had her as a teacher.

Sadly, Miss Cornett passed away in 2017 at age 90. Through the years since I was in those history classes with her, I often thought about trying to find her to tell her how much I appreciated all she had done for me and for taking me aside and calmly giving me life-changing advice. As mentioned, I didn't take her advice right away, but in the end, I did listen to her. I never did look for her to thank her, and I should have. But life got in the way, and I thought there would always be time for that later. That's not an excuse, I should have made the time to see her before she passed, and I feel bad about that. I think about her often and all the help and attention she gave me 35 years ago. She never got to know the difference she made in my life, at least not to the degree I know it.

To all the teachers out there, you may not always think you are affecting some of your students in a positive way, but you are.

College, a New Baby And Poverty

I went to college late in life, at the age of 28. In the fall of 1990, I started a three-year Computer Science program at Seneca College. A few months earlier, in July, we found out Nancy was going to have our first child. Our daughter, Grace, was born in early 1991, midway into my second semester at college.

I faced harassment by some family and so-called close friends leading up to the start of school. There were a lot of comments about how I shouldn't go to school and that I should be getting a job to support my family instead. Prior to this, my employment history was a series of dead-end jobs and I had tried a lot of different fields. I tried to become a police officer, a firefighter, a paramedic, and a stockbroker, but none of those careers worked out. I didn't listen to those people, who told me I shouldn't go to school, and I ended up going full time while working 20 hours a week with almost 20 hours a week of homework – it was insane.

Even though I worked almost every weekend, we were still quite poor. We were happy, though, and we made it through each week. Grace was such a good baby and I loved her so much I couldn't wait to get home every day to see her.

The years of working and attending college were difficult, but we muddled through it all. When Grace was a toddler, we lived in a cockroach-infested apartment on South Kingsway where we paid $600 a month. Each morning the three of us would drive five miles in heavy city traffic to Nancy's job in downtown Toronto. Her job was located at the foot of Bay

Street close to where you could catch the ferry to the Toronto Islands, at an advertising agency that had a daycare located in the building. The daycare was run by George Brown College, so we got the best of care for Grace.

After dropping them off, I would drive almost 15 miles up the Don Valley Parkway (DVP) to Seneca College. I would attend my classes and then drive 30 miles to Mississauga and work three or four hours depending on what time classes ended. Then I would drive another 18 miles back home to Swansea. At night I would do my homework for a minimum of two hours, though sometimes as many as four. On the days I had to work, Nancy and Grace would take the bus and subway home. On the days I didn't work, I would drive downtown from school and pick them up and we traveled home together. The next day we would do it all over again.

We were living in total abject poverty at the time, but I needed to finish school by any means necessary, and Nancy supported me throughout. Other than a small government study grant I got the first year of college, we had no financial support from family or any more money from the government. There were days when we didn't have enough gas for me to make it to school or downtown so I stayed home and completed homework, while Nancy and Grace would take public transit to work and daycare. There were other times when we had just enough gas in the car for me to drive them downtown and head back home and I would have to miss school. Eventually, I would make up time for the days I missed and that was an additional burden added to my already crushing homework schedule.

At that time, we were barely surviving. The minimum withdrawal allowed at a bank machine was five dollars, and any balances below that were not accessible. On more than one occasion, we needed milk, or food, but only had three dollars or a little more in the bank, so we had no access to that small amount of money. To get around this hurdle, I would deposit a two-dollar bill into my account at the bank machine. This was when there was still two-dollar paper money in Canada. This transaction would put the account balance over the minimum of five dollars needed for withdrawal and I would withdraw the five dollars so I could go and buy the milk or whatever other groceries we needed.

The combined stresses of no money, coupled with working, school, and no sleep was incredible, but we got through it – somehow, we got through.

I have always been aware of the passage of time, and there is an aside in the story called, "I Don't Believe You," earlier in the book about The Corner Bench. In that aside story, I say, "Strangely, I did know it at the time, I knew that time would end, and it all ended too soon – way too soon." I am constantly thinking of the end of things, good or bad. Meaning I do think a lot about how all things come to an end at some point, as in, "This too shall pass."

One afternoon while I drove home after a grueling day of exams, I was exhausted. The exhaustion was not only from the full-time college course load, but also from living my life with my wife, taking care of my new child, and working like crazy on top of living in poverty. All of it together was taking a lot out of me. I had exited the DVP onto the Gardiner Expressway. The Gardiner is an elevated highway that runs through the bottom part of the city, and I could see all the downtown skyscrapers on the right. From the west, the light of the gleaming late-day sun bouncing off the steel and glass buildings made the whole city core look like an orange, futuristic movie scene. I looked over and thought, *After I finish school, there's room for me there – if I'm able to finish. You've got to keep going, Todd. At some point, the day will come when the difficult times will be over.* I believed I would finish school and be able to get a good paying job.

At that time, I had finished writing the final exams of the fourth semester of the six-semester Computer Science program. This meant I now qualified for the two-year diploma if I wanted to stop school, and I was seriously considering doing that. I wasn't sure how much more I could take. These thoughts occurred in the spring of 1992, when I was 29. I had already signed up to go to school for the fifth semester in the summer session, then finish up the sixth and final semester for the three-year program in December. I did that because I wasn't sure I would be able to continue for another full year, time and money-wise. And of course, I wasn't sure if I could take it mentally. Signing up for the summer semester meant I would be enrolled for four straight semesters in a row, with no break. It was a difficult decision, but I had to do it.

On that last day of exams, I told a close friend of mine, who was in the same program with me at Seneca, though 10 years younger, that I was thinking of quitting and not returning to school. He was concerned and told me he thought I should stick it out and continue. I remember a little of that short conversation, not the details, but he told me to continue, and that I could do it. As I drove home that day, I wasn't sure if I could, and was strongly thinking of quitting school and taking the two-year diploma.

I learn quickly, but college challenged me like nothing ever had before. The workload was incredible; it was unlike anything I had ever experienced, and I was not mentally prepared for it. I had worked extremely hard up to this point with many, many long days and there were times when I continually worked 60-hour weeks back-to-back without a break before college. College was knocking me out and I was barely getting through it.

I was young, in good physical condition, and always paid attention to my diet, so none of that was an issue. The time I was spending in the car for my daily commute, as well as my lack of sleep, was starting to get to me. There was too much all at once and I almost never had a break. I was having a difficult time keeping up, and my schoolwork was starting to be affected.

During that exam period, I had an early morning English exam, which was worth 40% of the final mark. It was an open book exam about *The Scarlet Letter* by Nathaniel Hawthorne.

I was never a fast reader, and I hadn't read this book before. The book was almost three hundred pages and I had no choice but to stay up most of the night before the exam to read it. I was able to get through about three quarters of it before I had to stop and get some sleep. I was hoping that what I had read would be enough.

On the morning of the exam, I was tired, but since it was an open book exam, and I had it all fresh in my mind, I whipped through the exam in no time. After the exam, I promptly drove home and slept for the rest of the day and through the night. I scored a 90% on the exam, which resulted in a final grade of 84% for the course, but I never did that again.

I had about a month to make up my mind before the summer semester started. When I got home and told Nancy how I was feeling, she told me to relax, get some rest, and try to wind down for a week before making a final decision. She told me she would support me in any decision. During all these hard times she had supported me, she had also taken care of our baby and the household when I wasn't home; she was also working a full-time job. It wasn't an easy time for her either.

When it was close to the time to return to school for the summer semester, I had calmed down a bit, gotten some rest, and decided to try and finish out the three-year diploma program straight through. One of the reasons I decided to go back was I knew it would end – school would end. Another reason was I knew that time would pass; I had no control over that. What I did have control over was what I would have achieved when that time had passed. At the end, I would have either the two-year or the three-year diploma. It was up to me and nobody else.

Eventually, I completed the three-year diploma program. To achieve it, I pretty much didn't sleep for the two years and three months I was in school. After I graduated, I was so burned out I couldn't even look at a computer. I barely got off the couch for three weeks afterwards.

I have always thought about life in this way – time moves on. It's what you do with that time that matters. I have found that thinking about and accepting that fact helps you get through the difficult times that may come up in life. Unfortunately, it works both ways – good times also end. Of the two, sometimes I feel it is the loss of the good times that is harder to deal with than going through difficult times.

After I recovered from school, I started to look for a job in the computer field. This was right before the internet hit, so there was no widespread use of email. I wrote up a good resume and cover letter, mailed out 300 resumes, and got over 150 rejection letters. I still have those rejection letters. By the third month I was starting to get depressed and began thinking it was all a big waste of time. I kept running a printing press while looking for a computer programming job, but I hated it so much, I could only do it part time.

In the middle of April 1993, I got a call for an interview. It was the only computer programming job interview I got, but it was in Markham, which is far north and east of downtown Toronto and coincidentally about seven miles farther north from the Seneca College campus I had attended. I went to the interview and was offered the job. I was happy, and I loved the job, though I hated the commute. The office culture was like IBM in the mid-1960s, all white shirts and ties, which I also hated. The atmosphere was stuffed shirt and always so serious, but I was learning, and getting paid, even though it was less money than my printing press job. I figured I could stick it out for about a year to 18 months, before trying to get a better and higher paying job downtown.

Getting the job downtown is what happened, but not on my own accord. We had another baby in spring of 1994 when my son Jake was born, and at that time, I asked my boss for a raise. That request was not well-received and a few weeks later he fired me with some bullshit excuse that I was making too many mistakes and that the customers were complaining about my work. Strangely, I had never heard about any of these complaints during the 18 months I had worked there prior to asking for the raise.

A few months later, I did get that job in downtown Toronto, and I went to work in one of the big shiny office towers. My real computer programming career had finally begun. With my new job, my family could start to build the better life we had been waiting so long and working so hard for.

That first computer job downtown was the first time I had any real responsibility, a job where a lot of people relied on me. Most of the time, I was the only one who had the responsibility for fixing things and making sure the system I was working on was up and running, and running correctly. This was something I had never had before. I would have problems I was solely responsible for, and at first, I felt overwhelmed and not sure if I could handle it all. It was causing me stress, and I would go home at night thinking, *There is no way I can fix this. I have no idea what it is, or how to fix it*. This went on for a long time, until one day I thought to myself, *Just because you don't have the answer right now, doesn't mean you won't work it out. Just like all the other times you did.*

The next day, I went into work and fixed the issue. After that, I never had doubts about my abilities, and my confidence had risen to a new level. Now I always think in that way, and as a result, I have much less stress and I always figure out the problem.

Never Judge a Book By Its Cover I

When I was in my mid-30s, I worked as a computer programmer in the city. This was in the mid-90s and the market was hot for computer people before the dot-com crash of 2000. I was getting calls from headhunters for contracts with a lot of Fortune 500 companies all the time, and as time went by, the money offered kept getting better and better. I had good contracts that paid well, were in good locations, and provided work I enjoyed, so I didn't jump around much.

During this time, I lived in the condominiums in South Swansea, and I was married with two kids under the age of 10. I used to frequent the Swansea Plaza a lot since it was right beside us, and I could walk there for anything I needed.

One beautiful Saturday afternoon, I was at the plaza in the little convenience store run by a nice guy named Stewart and his wife. I would take my children there often and let them buy any candy they wanted.

While I was waiting around for the kids to grab their candy, I made small talk with Stewart. I walked to the back of the store to get some ice cream from the freezer, and on my way back to the front I saw a man walk into the store, who I recognized as a boy from my childhood.

Dan was a few years older than me, and I never hung out with him in my youth, but I knew him, and he knew me. I was surprised to see Dan, he left the neighbourhood 15 or 20 years earlier and I hadn't seen him since.

I was looking a little disheveled in a pair of old jeans and a t-shirt. I'd had the previous day off, after working five grueling 12 hour days straight. I had a few days growth of beard, and I was not looking like top management material.

Dan was just paying for a pack of smokes as I was walking to the front of the store. With a big smile I stuck out my hand and said, "Dan, long time no see. How the heck are ya?"

Dan shook my hand, and said in a condescending manner, "Bueler? What are you doing now, selling dope?" He said this right in front of my children. At first I thought he was kidding, but he didn't laugh or act like it was a joke. I was a little taken aback and said, "Nope, I'm a computer programmer downtown." He looked me up and down and said, "Sure you are," then turned and walked out of the store. I was shocked to say the least. *What a jerk,* I thought to myself.

My son was too young to understand what was going on, but my little girl was attuned to things happening around her. While standing beside me, she looked up and asked who that man was and why he was so rude to me. I told her he was an old Swansea friend as I ruffled her hair and she said, "Oh, okay, Dad."

When we got home, my daughter emphatically said, "But Dad, you never told me why your old friend was so rude to you in the store!" I explained to her what judging a book by its cover meant. She said, "So, Dad, does that mean you were the book?"

"Yes," I told her, "that's what it means."

She looked up at me and said, "Well, that's not nice."

"No," I told her, "no, it isn't."

I never saw Dan again after that day.

The Joys of Having Children

Before they tore down the Swansea Plaza on Southport Street, I lived in the condominiums half a block north. I used to take my son to the little convenience store in the plaza sometimes.

One day when my son was eight, we were coming home from an outing, and we stopped in the store so I could buy him some candy. It was summer, and we had an old '75 Jeep CJ5 at the time with the top completely off and no doors. After we got the candy and were driving the short distance home, Jake could not wait to start eating his candy. He asked me if he could have some now and, of course, I said yes.

I had bought him a lot of candy that day, since he had been very good while we were out. He had all different types of candy of various textures, colours and sizes. He opened one package and had a few pieces, then he reached in to get some more and offered some to me. I said, "No, I'm good. Maybe I'll try some later."

Well, he looked at me like I had horns coming out of my head. His big blue eyes, long, almost white-blonde hair blowing in the wind, and his cute little face were just staring up at me. He was genuinely concerned for me. He said, "Dad, are you okay?" I laughed, ruffled his hair, and told him yes, I was fine. As quickly as his expression had turned to concern, it went away with a shrug. "Okay!" he said, and just continued eating his candy as we drove home.

It really is all about the little things that sometimes last just a few seconds that people miss if they don't take the time to notice. I'll never forget that day, or Jake's cute little face, his concern, and his utter amazement when I turned down the candy.

Never Judge a Book By Its Cover II

One Saturday when I was in my early 30s, I went downtown to get my hair cut. I came home and looked in the mirror and for some reason, I thought it was too short, I didn't like it. It made my head and face look huge. I never wore my hair short, just short enough to satisfy the office environment where I worked.

I told Nancy I didn't like the cut and that it was bothering me. She said it looked fine. In fact, she said I could keep it that short all the time, it was fine with her. She said it would grow out in a few weeks anyway. That was a nice thing for her to say, and I felt she was being sincere when she said it. But it still bothered me.

Later that afternoon, we went up to the Bloor Meat Market east of Windermere Avenue on the south side of Bloor Street, to get some nice steaks for dinner. Behind the meat counter there is a large mirror that started about shoulder height and ran the whole length of the store. While we were waiting for our turn to order, I could not stop looking at myself in the mirror and what I felt was my awful haircut.

Our turn came to order and Nancy spoke to the butcher about what would be best for four people for steaks. She bought some other meats too.

There were two women beside us who were next in line. I noticed they were both staring at me and seemed to have disgusted looks on their faces. I was self-conscious about my haircut and how I looked, and them staring at me made my anxiety about it worse. This made me look in the mirror at myself even more.

We got our meat, paid, and left the store. All that time, the two women were staring at me. I asked Nancy after we left if she had seen the two women, and did she notice that they were looking at me the whole time. She said she had and she overheard them say, "Look at this guy. He keeps looking at himself in the mirror. If he doesn't stop, I'm leaving. Sheesh, what a narcissist!" I never heard them as they were on Nancy's side and I was closer to the back of the store.

I said, "Really? Why didn't you say something?" Nancy knew I was looking in the mirror because I was self-conscious about my hair, and had told me twice to stop looking in the mirror, saying "Your hair is fine." She thought it was funny what the women thought. In the end, I guess it was.

But it just goes to show, you don't know what is going on with people you don't know, sometimes even people you do know. It's best to reserve judgment until you do. Never judge a book by its cover.

My Dad

Pong

My father was a computer programmer starting in the mid-1950s. He wasn't much of a consumer product technology guy, though he did bring home some new technology items he thought were cool. We had one of the first pocket calculators and I got one of those tiny, tiny radios about 2"x 2" with one little tiny ear bud for Christmas one year.

One day in 1972 when I was 10, my dad brought home the Pong game. Pong was the very first home video game you could buy, and he was quite excited about it. I had a friend over that Saturday afternoon watching wrestling or OHA hockey. My dad hooked up the Pong game to our TV and we started to play.

We played for about an hour as my dad watched, laughed, and tried to teach us the best way to score points. I was not interested in the game for some reason. So we played a little bit longer, then my bud and I said we were bored and went out to the Rec Centre. I thought my dad would be disappointed, but he wasn't at all. That was the first and last video game I ever played. Well, I have played some for a few minutes here and there, but not for more than that. For some reason I was never into playing video games. To this day, I don't understand what people get out of playing them; it never appealed to me.

One Froggy Evening

The cartoon *One Froggy Evening* would come on some Saturday mornings in the early 70s. My dad would be reading the huge Saturday paper while my mom was out doing the weekly grocery shopping. On the days I didn't go shopping with my mom, I would be about 12 inches from the TV, sitting on the floor while eating my bowl of Sugar Frosted Flakes. And yes, I was wearing my cowboy pajamas. My dad would laugh and laugh when the cartoon would come on.

He'd say, "This guy just can't catch a break!" As a kid, I only half got what my dad meant. But I now see that my dad, as a full grown adult with a house, four kids, and a high stress job, had much more insight into the innocent cartoon.

Sometimes I wonder how difficult life was for my dad in those days. I'm thinking it was hard. But he did it. Married with four kids, the car breaking down, working 60 hour weeks many times, and all the other problems of modern life in the 70s. All with no internet, no computers in the house, no cellphones, no answering machines, no banking cards or ATMs. And he did it day after day, month after month, year after year.

Those few short hours he had to relax on Saturday mornings were the only times he had a break.

Other Writings

Leaving School at 15

Leaving school at 15 wasn't all my decision. It was a combination between me and the adults around me at the time, and it was a pivotal point in my life. The consequences of what happened then drove just about every single aspect of the rest of my life, even now, more than 45 years later. I ended up chasing that missing education for more than 15 years after I first left high school. I did eventually achieve a college education, which cost me dearly. Not only in lost money, but lost time, at a young age I sometimes feel was unnecessarily wasted.

It still affects me and everyone close to me, even at over 60 years of age. I still have recurring dreams about what happened all those years ago. In one dream I am trying to get to a final exam I hadn't studied for and in no way could have passed. I am running around my old high school, desperately trying to get to the exam. In the dream, in the end, I miss the exam. It is a very traumatic dream. And when I am jolted from the dream in the middle of the night, I find myself shaking. I must also say, I am happy that I am able to now, after all these years, get all of this out of my head. Has writing this book stopped the dreams? Unfortunately no, I am still plagued by them to this day. I don't know if they will ever stop. But maybe this book can serve as a warning to others to try to do their best possible to make the right decisions in life, and not to let others dictate your decisions for you. If you don't make the right decisions, it may affect your life forever, even if at the time it does not seem significant.

If there are any young people reading this book, I strongly advise against leaving school early in life. Stay in school as long as you can; you'll thank your younger self later. Hindsight, though, is easier than foresight. I understand that, and I have learned that the hard way.

1980 April Wine Concert Ticket

High Strangeness in Swansea

I was up early one morning in late April of 2023 working on this book. I had just finished the 1980 April Wine concert story a few days prior, and I always go through my big stories maybe ten times or more to make sure everything is correct.

I have an incredible memory for events and details of those events, even 40 or 50 years later. But some memories are completely gone. I still speak with a friend from the old Swansea days, and during our talks, she sometimes brings up old things that happened of which I have absolutely no recollection.

While I go through my stories, I want to make sure my memory is correct. Little things, like making sure all the timelines add up, who was there, and what, where, and when I did something all matter. I can't always get everything perfect, so sometimes if the story allows for it, I use the internet or talk with others to try to get the continuity of the story correct the best I can.

That morning I was going through the concert story, and I knew from when I was writing the story, there was an opening act for April Wine that night. However, I couldn't remember who the act was. It didn't bother me too much at the time I was writing the story, as I wanted to get all the memories out of my head and into the old iPhone I write on. I figured I could always look into it later. That morning in late April was the day to look into it.

I started by doing some internet research on who the opening act was that night at Maple Leaf Gardens. I know there was an opening act, we had gotten our tickets from scalpers after the concert had already started, and when we got to our seats, it wasn't April Wine up on stage. It didn't take me long to find out the opening act was Johnny Winter. Now, I have no memory at all of his set in any way. He apparently didn't play a long set that night, and I only remember April Wine coming on stage. So I had completed the continuity for that small issue in the story.

Now, here's the strange part!

While I was searching the internet about the concert, I wanted to know about Johnny Winter's set to see if that would spark any memory of it. But no, nothing. That was okay, it wasn't pertinent to the story, only for my own peace of mind. As I was searching about Johnny Winter, though, a link popped up on my computer screen from eBay. The small thumbnail on the link looked familiar to me, so I clicked on it. It was for a ticket stub for the concert in my story. *Well*, I thought to myself, *that's strange*. But as I looked closer at the photos of the ticket stub on the eBay auction, I was stunned to find it was my ticket stub from that night. How did I know it was mine? Well, I have always kept every ticket stub from every concert I ever went to. But about 20 years prior, for some reason the market for old concert ticket stubs was pretty high, and some were going for good money. So I sold about four or five of my old stubs at the time for a good price. I never sold my Rolling Stones stub, or the stub from the first concert I ever went to, which was Triumph, but I sold my April Wine stub.

Not only that, but there was writing on the top of the stub that said, "Johny Winter." I remember that being on my stub, and the stub was for gold seats which was what we got from the scalper at the time.

I can't remember if I wrote that on the stub or not. My handwriting has changed over the past 45 years, but it did look like my handwriting from the time. And I've never been the greatest speller on the planet.

You can see Johnny is misspelled on the stub. So I could have written that on the stub. Of course it could have been the scalper.

I'll never know. So I bought the ticket stub from the auction, (See concert ticket photos).

I was having a discussion with Nancy about this ticket stub right after I bought it back; she was my girlfriend at the time of the concert. She seemed to think "Johny Winter" is in her handwriting, but I think it's mine. She is, and always has been a terrific speller, so I don't think she would have misspelled "Johny" on the stub at the time. Then I noticed someone wrote "sucks" beside April Wine on the stub. And that looks more like female handwriting to me. Could it be that I wrote "Johny Winter," and Nancy wrote "sucks" later, to bug me? Yes, it could be.

Writing this book has been an interesting experience. After more than 45 years, a small memento of a great night returned to me through a serendipitous coincidence.

The Brain Tumour Incident

Here's the skinny on the brain tumour:

What I have is called a colloid cyst. About three people in a million have it. You can look it up if you're interested. It's a liquid-filled cyst right smack dab in the middle of my head. My neurosurgeon says I've probably had it since I was about 14 years old. I didn't even know I had it, and this is how I found out.

In the fall of 2019, I was riding my bike on the north side of The Queensway, almost right in front of St. Joe's hospital in Toronto, with no helmet, on my way to Roncesvalles. I crossed Sunnyside, the street that runs north and south beside St. Joe's, and tried to hop up the curb on the other sidewalk. But I didn't make it and the front wheel hit the curb and I went over the handlebars. My head hit the concrete sidewalk. I was knocked out for a few seconds, and when I woke up I was on the ground with blood running down my face. A young lady was standing over me. She asked if I was okay and I said I didn't know. She said she saw me fall and that I had blood running down my face. I reached up to touch my face, felt the blood, then looked at my hand and saw the blood. I felt okay, though a little disoriented. She told me I should go to the hospital and get checked out. I said I would and asked her if she knew where a hospital was. She looked a little stunned, and then she told me "Right there," while pointing to St. Joe's not 25 feet away. I said thanks, then took my bike and walked over to the emergency department.

When I got called up to triage, the clerk asked me for my name. To my surprise, I didn't know. So they asked if I had a wallet on me. I did and I gave it to them. They found my driver's licence and my OHIP – Ontario provincial health insurance – card. They put all the info into their computer and told me to wait. By this time I had stopped bleeding.

After waiting in triage, I was seen by a doctor and they asked me my name again. This time, I answered correctly, but they wanted to do a CT scan on my head to check things out just in case. I had the scan done quickly and the doctor came back about a half hour later to talk to me. He said everything was fine but I did have a colloid cyst and he asked me if I knew I had it. I told him no, and that I had no idea what a colloid cyst even was. The doctor told me it was a kind of brain tumour. I was a little taken aback by this news, but he told me it wasn't big and it wasn't malignant. That made me feel a little better. They then made an appointment for me with a neurosurgeon for a month later so they could look at it more closely.

The day of my appointment with the neurosurgeon I got an MRI, and the neurosurgeon came to talk to me afterwards. He told me the tumour is small, six millimeters, and then he started to tell me the details about what it is. This is when I started to get a little freaked out. After telling me what little I already knew, he told me about the bad stuff. He told me the tumour could block the fluid that your brain sits in from properly circulating. If this happens before you can get to the hospital to get it fixed, the blockage could cause a heart attack. You have about 24 hours before you die without medical intervention. So if you get a really bad headache, you need to get to a hospital as quickly as possible.

I asked the doctor how do I know when this happens, if it does? He told me I would get a very bad headache. I asked him how I would be able to tell the difference between a regular headache and a very bad headache? He said it would be the worst headache I've ever had. "You'd know," he said. And when could this happen? He said it could happen at any moment with no way of knowing in advance.

Then I asked him what if it was to happen while I was sleeping? He said the pain would wake me up for sure. At this point, I was really scared and I started to cry.

Then, as plain and as matter-of-fact as can be – and I can't fault him for this, as I'm sure he's seen a lot worse – he looked at me and said, "Todd, these are the cards you've been dealt in life. You just need to pay attention."

So, I said, "Okay, Doc, thanks." He told me I needed to come and have an MRI every year. Then I asked him if it could be removed, and he said yes, it was up to me. If I wanted it removed, he could do that, but right now the risk of removing it is much higher than leaving it in.

I've now been going for an MRI every year since and everything is fine; there has been no growth. I have now started to look more into the condition. Almost everyone who has this condition doesn't know they have it as there are no symptoms until there are. And by the time you get symptoms, you have 24 hours, sometimes less, to get to a hospital. If you don't go to the hospital and you don't know you have the colloid cyst, you could have a heart attack, and unless there is some reason to do an autopsy, they would never know you died from the colloid cyst that caused the heart attack, and not a normal heart attack. It's pretty spooky stuff.

So I may have lived almost my whole life with this thing in my head I never knew I had, and it could have killed me at any time, with no real warning other than a very bad headache. And everyone would have thought I had died from a normal heart attack. Crazy, eh?

At first I wanted the cyst out of my head. But as time has gone by, I've realized it is better to leave it in and go on living my life. If something happens, then I know what to do. So that is how I live my life now. I used to think about it every day, every week, every month. Now I almost never think about it and it doesn't bother me in the least.

The Postman Gets Knocked Down Twice – Why Write It?

I had a short conversation with my wife about the postman story while we were editing it together one Sunday morning, November 28, 2021. This was before I posted it to social media.
She asked me, "Why write this story?"
"Well," I said, "I could break it down to its simplest form. Which would be, I once had a job as a postman, and I got attacked by a dog."

But who cares about that? Who wants to read about that? Boring. The thing is, nobody cares about how I had a job as a postman; other than meeting nice people who you deliver to, it's a boring job. And while getting attacked by a dog is surely not boring, who wants to hear, "Ya, I once got attacked by a dog."

But to tell the story, it needed to be expanded on from just the one sentence. To make it interesting, you need to tell the story, as it happened.

Something happened that I wasn't expecting when I posted this story to social media. Some people said the story was riveting, terrifying, disturbing, but also exciting. I didn't mean to upset anyone. I don't know what I expected would happen when people read the story. I never know until I put it out there. Since this story actually happened, should I have known the reaction would be different from the reaction to a fictional story? Maybe.

Here's the strange thing. While I was writing the story, I wasn't thinking, *Is this too scary for people? Am I going to traumatize anyone?* All I thought while writing was, *Is this good? Will people feel like they are right beside me? Will this make people want to keep reading?*

You'd think I would be traumatized by it, but I'm okay. I guess I should be, but it was a long time ago. Although I remember it vividly, I don't have any PTSD over it. But I have been cautious around dogs since that day – not afraid, but cautious.

I needed to tell that story, my story, my experience. I needed to tell that story as it happened to me, in all the raw, gritty detail. I needed to bring the reader beside me, while it was happening. I wanted the reader to be right there with me, beside me, experiencing what I had experienced, without having to actually go through it, without the real-life terror. I wanted the reader to feel like I felt at the time, while knowing they were safe on their couch, or in bed reading, with their heart pounding. That's what a story is. Like riding a roller coaster, real danger right there in front of you, but no real danger. And for the residents of Swansea, past and present, I want everyone to think, *Hey, I was there, I've been right at that place where that happened, I feel a connection.* That's why I wrote the story. That's why I write all my stories; to make connections, and to evoke emotions. I hope I have been able to achieve all that and more with the stories I have shared.

The End

Well, that's it. I think I have said just about everything I wanted to say, for now. All good things come to an end. But there are always new beginnings, new friends, and new adventures to explore.

Photo – Ursula Fey

Appendix A
The Coochie Dome

This first section here is the history of the game of Coochie, and the Coochie Dome, as told to the author by Bruce Dunstan:

The game of Coochie was invented in Rennie Park by an individual who did not live in Swansea, but he was friends with many people who lived there. His name was John Kutchaluma (sp.), also known as Cooch. He went to Runnymede Public School in the 1960s and Western Tech High School in the early 1970s.

John and I became friends through a mutual friendship, and he met his wife through a girl I knew while we were at her house.

John was a large man and I remember going to Jamaica with him. For those who remember John, he could swim like a fish and was a great guy whom I remember fondly.

Soon after the picnic gazebo was built in Rennie Park, Cooch came up with an idea for a game we could play in the dome using a basketball, though we settled on a different ball in the end.

John's invented game has been played for many years, and it lives on to this very day.

A description of the Coochie Dome and how the game was played when I was a boy

The Coochie Dome, or picnic gazebo, was built in 1966 and still stands today at the south end of Rennie Park. It's built on a large round concrete base, with eight concrete pillars holding up the wooden roof. The roof is covered with shingles and the ceiling consists of wooden slats. The dome itself is about 25–30 feet tall. Each of the eight pillars is 8.5 feet tall and it is 40 feet across from one side to the other. The circumference is 120 feet.

The game was played with a red rubber ball that was similar in size and texture to a dodgeball. The neighbourhood kids

Appendix A

quickly dubbed it a Coochie ball. These balls had a lot of bounce to them, and those who have played the game know that the ball makes a distinctive and loud metallic *ping* sound when it hits something. As mentioned in other stories in this book, we could always grab one of these balls from the park's clubhouse, along with almost any ball or sports equipment we needed.

The game did not have a limit of players. Each player was assigned a number to let them know in which order they played. The first player would "serve" the ball by hitting, kicking, throwing, or even head-butting the ball to the top or sides of the dome's interior. When the ball came down, the next player – by their assigned number – would have only two bounces to keep the ball in play by getting the ball back up to the top or sides of the dome's interior. The round would continue until someone missed or didn't hit the ball within two bounces.

When there was a large group of players, sometimes a player would get confused and forget it was their turn. The ball would just bounce with no one stepping up to play. No one would say anything to that player, and they would get a strike against them. Sometimes they would realize they were missing their turn at the last second and they'd attempt to play the ball and miss; that was entertaining. When there were larger groups of players, it was best to remember which player had the number just before yours so you would be ready to play when it was your turn.

If the ball bounced three times on the ground before you hit it back up to the ceiling, that was one strike; if you got three strikes, you were out of the game. Notably, the number three was significant in this game. It took three bounces to equal one strike, and three strikes to equal being kicked out of the game. If you got hit by the ball, even if it wasn't your turn, that was a strike against you. The game would continue until there was one player left – the winner.

Appendix B
True or False Answers Part I

1. False. Although I did play in the pipe rink, I never got my foot caught, or needed to be cut free.

2. False. Not specifically for my feet, but I have made a bit of money over the last 30 years or so as a model, mainly in print ads.

3. True. We were riding his mini bike in the boy's yard on the east side of the school and in the schoolyard field. My bud said, "Let's try to go inside the school."
"I'm pretty sure the door is locked," I said.
But I tried it, and to our surprise, it was open. I held the door open, and he rode the mini bike right up the middle set of stairs where the office is. We then started taking turns riding the mini bike up and down the whole length of the hallway for about an hour.

4. True. I went straight home after throwing up and never made it back to the dance.

5. False. It didn't happen. I drank the Cosmopolitan before my mother found it... just kidding. It did not happen at all; it's an old joke. I think I got it from *Playboy* magazine. I will say this: if it did happen, my dad's response is something my father would have said for sure. My dad had a great sense of humour.

Appendix C
True or False Answers Part II

1. False. I was never arrested, detained, or held, but I did see the queen in High Park that day.

2. True. The wisdom teeth have pushed forward a little over the years, making my teeth a little crowded.

3. True. I went to see an ear, nose, and throat specialist as an adult and was told I may have had the deviated septum since I was a teenager. There is no real way to tell how long I have had it, or why I have it.

4. True. It is more of a risk to remove the tumour than to leave it in.

5. True. I trained for over two years. Other than going to college as an adult and writing this book, the NYC Marathon was one of the most difficult things I have done in my life.

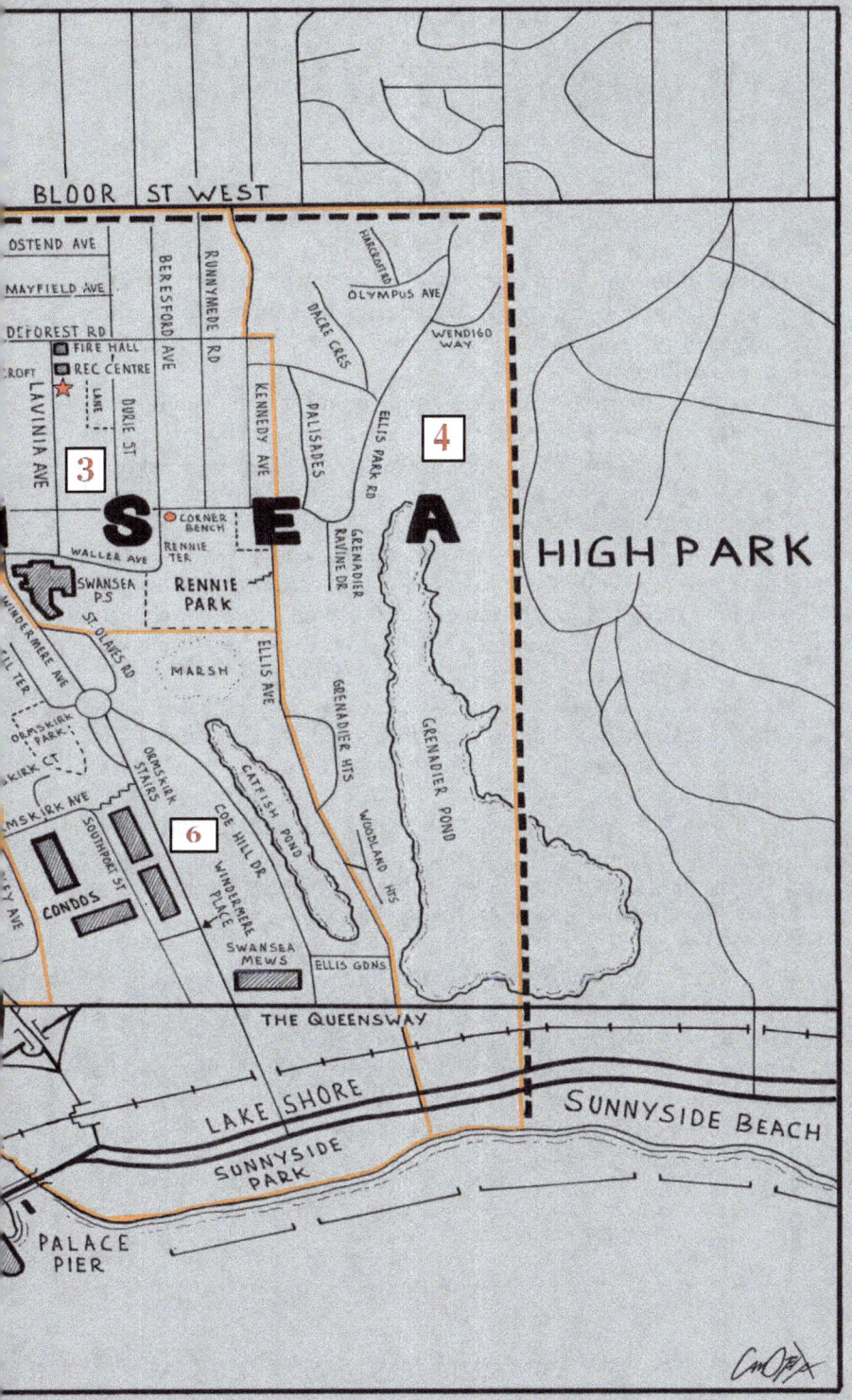

Appendix D
Micro Neighbourhoods

People think Swansea is just one neighbourhood. While that is true, the fact is Swansea is made up of a bunch of smaller neighbourhoods inside the main one. Each has its own distinct micro culture.

I grew up in the Main Grid and lived most of my adult life in South Swansea. There is a certain snobbishness about the Main Grid, and at times in my youth, I was ignorant of it. As I've grown older and wiser, I've realized that the way I felt in my younger years about exactly where I lived has all gone away.

In my less mature days, I had a short conversation with an older woman while shopping on Bloor Street one day. For some reason, though I can't remember the context, we exchanged where we lived. She told me she was from Riverside. I said, "Oh, I live in Swansea."

She said, "You know, Riverside is in Swansea." It was the first time I realized I had never thought about it all that much. After that conversation, I never thought of Swansea the same way as I had before.

I have had conversations with people in the Main Grid when I lived in the Southport condos, which are in South Swansea. When they asked me where I lived, of course I told them Swansea. "Where in Swansea?" was the next question.

My answer was, "The condos."

"That's not really Swansea," came the reply.

The differences in the micro neighbourhoods are not that big, though I would say they are noticeable. I have heard from many people that if you didn't grow up in or live in the Main Grid, that you're not really a Swansea person. While I don't agree with that, I can see how people would think this way.

Those micro neighbourhoods have never been properly named. So I've coined the names and lay out the borders here.

Appendix D

1. Riverside
Pretty self-explanatory, also includes Brûlé.

2. Armadale
South Kingsway north of Morningside to Bloor, and all streets east of South Kingsway.

3. Main Grid or Main Central Grid
Waller to the south, Bloor to the north. Windermere to the west, Kennedy to the east. But this includes the school, the school hill, and Rennie Park. Also includes the streets west off Windermere but not going into the South Kingsway Valley. This is where all the main neighbourhood infrastructure is, including the school, Rennie Park, the Rec Centre, the town hall and library, and the fire hall.

4. Ellis/High Park
Ellis Avenue and all streets that pretty much border High Park.

5. South Kingsway
South Kingsway from The Queensway to Morningside, including the streets east of South Kingsway, but not the condos.

6. South Swansea
Anything south of the school in the middle of the neighbourhood. This doesn't include Ellis, South Kingsway, or Armadale, but does include the condos.

Appendix E
Swansea School Report Cards

These are actual verbatim transcriptions from the physical report cards. The picture below is my Kindergarten report card from 1967/1968.

Appendix E

Kindergarten – 1967/1968
Teacher – Miss A. Malcolm

December 1st Report
Todd has made an adjustment to kindergarten. He is a happy child at school who participates in most of the activities. At times he needs help to keep him listening and attending during conversation periods.

Todd is becoming aware of differences in sound and is able to reproduce tunes during singing period.

Todd is beginning to show an interest in the printed form in identifying his own and some classmates' names in print. He also notices that certain printed words begin the same.

Todd is able to fasten his outdoor clothing and willingly assists other children with difficulties.

March 15th Report
Todd has progressed during this term at school. He expresses himself in sentences when describing his activities and speaks so that he shows an understanding of numbers, order and quantity in using such words as circle, triangle, first, short, five, etc.

Todd has displayed leadership qualities and takes pride in being chosen to direct the children in routines, games, etc.

Todd prefers to work with toys at activity time and usually plays with one or two special friends. At times he needs help to keep him working constructively.

Todd is able to count to fourteen and recognizes these symbols in print. He has shown some interest in printing numerals.

June Report
Todd has been an active, enthusiastic member of the group during his year in kindergarten. Recently he has been quite outspoken and often needs to be reminded to wait his turn to express his ideas.

Todd has shown that he is capable of working well next year in grade one if he learns to channel his excitable nature into constructive pursuits.

Grade One – 1968/1969
Teacher – Miss A. Gorrie

December 1st Report
Todd is doing well in his reading program. He has a retainable mind and recalls "sight" words readily. His work in phonics is also very satisfactory. He tends to be careless in his printing and hand-work, sacrificing neatness, and even accuracy, to speed.

Todd shows good understanding of our mathematics to date. He is not always attentive however, and has difficulty showing the courtesy of listening to others. He seems rather tense at times.

Todd has much to contribute to group activities, but sometimes overlooks the equal rights of others.

March 15th Report
Todd continues to make good progress this term. He is doing well in his reading program, and with consistent effort could improve his present grades. Todd's work in mathematics indicates a good understanding of this subject.

However Todd continues to display nervous tenseness, and is often inattentive. He seems to be experiencing difficulty in lengthening his attention span, as required by the work of this term. He is making a greater effort to recognize the rights of others.

June Report
Todd has done well in his reading program this year. His work in phonics, especially, is above class average. In mathematics, he is doing average work.

His printing and handwork suffer from the speed at which he tries to work. This same haste sometimes leads to carelessness on his part.

Todd still needs to learn about self-discipline, and the consideration of the equal rights of others. However, he is becoming more attentive in class.

Grade Two – 1969/1970
Teacher – Miss C. Epplett

December 1st Report
Todd has a large sight vocabulary and is proficient in applying his knowledge of phonics to new words. He comprehends what he reads.

Todd is working at his level in mathematics and often works ahead on his own initiative. However, he occasionally has difficulty in refraining from aggressive behavior towards his classmates. He also tends to speak out of turn. Todd has shown more self-control in both these areas in recent weeks.

March 15th Report
Todd has a large speaking vocabulary and a good general knowledge background.

Todd's written work is usually quickly and carelessly done. However, he has shown some indication of applying himself more diligently.

His work in both reading and mathematics is satisfactory, but I don't feel he is working to the best of his ability.

June Report
Todd has continued to complete his work satisfactorily. However, I still feel that Todd could be doing better than average work. I hope Todd will apply himself more diligently next year in grade three.

Acknowledgments

I would like to thank everyone who was involved in putting together this book. Without them, this book would not be what it is today.

To my editors: I want to thank you for all the hard work you have done. For putting up with me and all my idiosyncrasies as I waffled back and forth with changes to the text. You're like the old BASF commercials; you don't write the story, you make the story better!

Thank you to Chris Higgins for writing the foreword. I also want to thank Chris for all his positive encouragement when we would speak from time to time during the writing of the book. Chris also taught me the importance of using tense correctly.

Thank you to Elizabeth Tranter for her professional advice regarding copyright issues and procedures.

Thank you to Deb Fisher and Fred Fisher for helping me get the details right with the layout of their childhood home for the Riverside Drive story.

Thanks to John Bolton for doing some great investigative work into my parents' house in Aurora where I lived in the early 1960s. Also his research into my childhood home at 85 Lavinia Avenue in Toronto. John's research, along with my memory and conversations with my parents in the early 1980s, formed the basis for my origin story.

Thank you to Bruce Dunstan for the background information on the inventor of the game of Coochie.

Thank you to Drew Horgan for his technical help refreshing my memory about how I fooled around with the phone back in my high school days when I wanted to skip class.

The End photo – Deforest Road looking east towards Durie Street, 1978. Courtesy of Ursula Fey.

I would like to thank all the people of Swansea, current and past residents. Without all your encouragement and support during this years long journey, this book would never have been written.

And finally, I would like to thank my wife Nancy for all the hard work she has done during the four long years of the writing of this book. Nancy spent hundreds of hours making constructive suggestions about the book's individual stories, as well as editing as we went along and proofreading the final text. She has been instrumental to what the book is today.

About The Author

Born in Toronto and leaving school at the tender age of 15, Todd worked in mostly factory settings throughout his teen years and into his 20s. He eventually remedied that situation earning a three year computer science diploma from Seneca College. He then worked as a programmer and analyst for 30 years before becoming a writer. When he's not writing, Todd plays his guitar, and works on his classic Jeep, "There's always nuts and bolts left over for some reason." Todd lives and writes in Swansea, Toronto.

www.ingramcontent.com/pod-product-compliance
Lightning Source LLC
Chambersburg PA
CBHW070757020526
44118CB00036B/1844